THE

WESTERN TOURIST

AND

EMIGRANT'S GUIDE

THROUGH THE STATES OF

OHIO, MICHIGAN, INDIANA, ILLINOIS, MISSOURI,
IOWA, AND WISCONSIN,

AND THE TERRITORIES OF

MINESOTA, MISSOURI, AND NEBRASKA.

BEING AN ACCURATE AND CONCISE DESCRIPTION OF

EACH STATE AND TERRITORY;

AND CONTAINING

THE ROUTES AND DISTANCES ON

THE GREAT LINES OF TRAVEL.

ACCOMPANIED WITH

A LARGE AND MINUTE MAP, EXHIBITING THE TOWNSHIP LINES OF THE UNITED STATES' SURVEYS, THE BOUNDARIES OF COUNTIES, AND THE POSITION OF CITIES, VILLAGES AND SETTLEMENTS, ETC., ETC.

NEW YORK:
PUBLISHED BY J. H. COLTON AND COMPANY,
NO. 172 WILLIAM STREET.
1855.

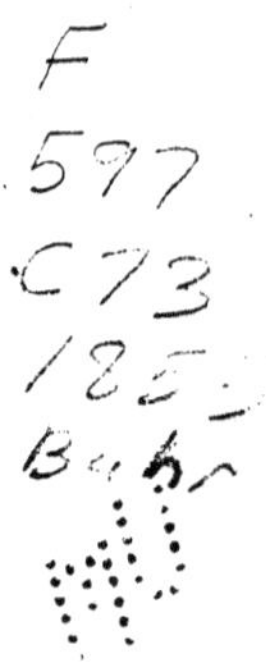

PUBLISHER'S ADVERTISEMENT.

THE great region of the North and West, comprehended in the states of Ohio, Michigan, Indiana, Illinois, Missouri, Iowa, and Wisconsin, and the territories of Minesota, Missouri, and Nebraska, is daily becoming more and more important and interesting. Its vast resources are in a state of rapid development. Industry and enterprise, aided by enlightened legislation, are calling forth its energies; and the prophetic declaration, that "*westward the star of empire takes its way*," is advancing to fulfilment. A few years ago this region, then denominated the "far west," was regarded as the outskirts of civilization—it is now (at least the greater portion of it) the residence of an active, vigorous, and intelligent population. The steamboat, railroad car, and telegraph have become its great movers. Cities have sprung up in the wilderness as if by the will of the magician; agriculture, manufactures, and commerce flourish; literature, science, and the arts are extending their healthful and invigorating influence throughout the country. Blessed with a soil unsurpassed in fertility, and a salubrious climate; and possessing, by means of its great rivers and lakes, advantages for trade and commerce, it enjoys all the influences that can render a country prosperous and a people happy.

The object of the present publication is to give a succinct account of the states and territories into which it is divided, and exhibit to the reader such information respecting their present condition and prospects as is necessary to a right understanding of the great interest of the region; and also to supply the public with a book of travel on which they may rely. Great experience, and no little expense have been employed in its compilation, and it is confidently anticipated that there will be found in its pages more extensive information, and a more accurate and far fuller list of *routes* than in any like publication. Both departments of the work have been compiled from entirely new material, and are adapted to the present state of things, and the extended facilities of travel by railroad, river, lake, canal, and stage-road.

Under the head of each state and territory will be found its respective boundaries and extent—its physical aspect—an account of its rivers, lakes, and internal improvements—its industry, as applied to the development of its resources—its natural products—its manufactures and commerce—its educational condition—descriptions of its chief cities, towns, and villages, and a sketch of its history and progress. This information is followed by "Tables of the Routes" in each state, which are indexed for convenience of reference.

To the tourist, commercial traveller, and emigrant such a work must be especially desirable,—embodying, as it does, a vast fund of information necessary for his convenience, and without which it is impossible to proceed understandingly on his journey.

The map accompanying this work has been carefully drawn from the government surveys. It exhibits the county and township lines; the location of cities and villages; and the tracks of railroads, canals, and post-roads, &c.; and is the most complete general map of the north-western states yet published.

CONTENTS.

CONTENTS.

INDEX TO THE ROUTES

THROUGH

THE WESTERN STATES.

INTRODUCTION.

That portion of the United States to which the designation of "Western States" is applied—the vast country delineated in this work—is occupied by the new and flourishing states of Ohio, Michigan, Indiana, Illinois, Missouri, Iowa, and Wisconsin, and the territories of Minesota, Missouri, and Nebraska. This immense region is situated between 36° 30′ and 49° N. lat., and between 80° 35′ and 114° W. long.: and is bounded N. by British America, and Lakes Superior, Huron, and Erie; E. by Pennsylvania and Virginia; S. by Kentucky, Arkansas, and the Indian Territory; and W. by the ridges of the Rocky Mountains. Exclusive of the area of the great lakes, the superficies of these states and territories is estimated to contain an area of 1,150,000 square miles.

The country within these limits is comprised in the two great valleys or basins of the St. Lawrence and Mississippi rivers.

The St. Lawrence Valley or Basin.—Regarding the St. Lawrence as a general name for the connected line of that great river or water system that unites with the Atlantic ocean in the Gulf of St. Lawrence, its remote source will be found to be the St. Louis river, an affluent of Lake Superior, rising in the table-land of Minesota territory, near the sources of the Mississippi and the Red river of the north. It receives different names in different parts of its course: being, as already seen, at first the St. Louis; between Lakes Superior and Huron it is the St. Mary; between Lakes Huron and Erie, the St. Clair and Detroit; between Lakes Erie and Ontario, the Niagara; and from Lake Ontario to Montreal it is called the Cataraqui or Iroquois; its course hence to the sea being the St. Lawrence, properly so called. Considered in this point of view, its entire course may be estimated at upwards of 2,000 miles. Lake Michigan, and also some smaller lakes, are included in the basin of this magnificent river—a basin containing an area of over 500,000 square miles, and enclosing the largest collection of fresh water to be found on the surface of the globe.

The source of the St. Louis is about 1,200 feet above the tide-level, but on account of falls and rapids, its elevation on reaching Lake Superior is only 641 feet. Lake Superior, the largest fresh-water lake in the world, has a length of 420 miles, and a mean breadth of 100 miles. Its average depth is 900 feet. Into this reservoir are poured upwards of 50 rivers, none of which, however, are of large size. The area of the basin of this lake is 90,000 square miles, one-third of which is covered by water. It forms the upper division of the great basin of the St. Lawrence, and is 45 feet more elevated than Lake Huron, and 410 feet more than Lake Ontario. The whole mass of these waters, composing a large river, is forced through the Strait of St. Mary, a distance of 60 miles, into Lake Huron. Sault St. Marie, a fall of 122 feet 10 inches in half a mile, is the largest of the rapids that obstruct navigation in this river.

The second or middle division of the basin contains Lakes Michigan, Huron, and Erie, and has an area of 160,000 square miles. The waters of these lakes rest in the lowest depressions of the section, and differ with themselves only 35 feet in elevation. Lake Michigan is 340 miles long, and in mean breadth 58 miles, and has an area of 10,000 square miles. Its elevation is 600 feet, and its mean depth 900 feet. This lake communicates with Lake Huron through the Strait of Mackinaw. Lake Huron is an expanded triangular body of water, divided into two unequal portions by the Manitoulin islands and a peninsula projecting from its southeast shore. The smaller and eastern portion of the lake thus separated is called Georgian Bay, and is 120 miles long, with an average breadth of 45 miles. The dimensions of Lake Huron are 270 miles long by 70 mean width. Its elevation is 596 feet, and its area 19,000 square miles. Besides the waters of Lakes Superior and Michigan, this lake receives a large number of streams from the N., E., and W. These accumulated waters are discharged from its southern extremity, by St. Clair river, into the small lake of the same name, and thence into Lake Erie by Detroit Strait. Lake Erie forms the most southern part of the middle section of the St. Lawrence basin. It is elevated 565 feet above tide-level, and 31 feet below the level of Lake Huron. Its form is elliptical, but much elongated, being 240 miles in length, and only about 38 in mean breadth. It is the shoalest of the great lakes—averaging only about 120 feet in depth.

The lower section of the basin now commences. The waters are precipitated over the Falls of Niagara, and after a course of 14 miles expand and form Lake Ontario, having by falls and rapids in the Niagara river made a descent of 334 feet, of which 164 are contributed by the great cataract. The area of this lake is 5,400 square miles, and its mean depth 492 feet. The length of Lake Ontario is 180 miles, and its average width 40 miles. At its eastern extremity the river proper begins, and after a course of 692 miles connects with the Atlantic. In magnitude it is the second river in America. It is 100 miles wide at its mouth, and navigable for the largest class of ships for 400 miles from the ocean.

The water surface of the whole basin of the St. Lawrence is about 73,000 square miles, and the solid contents of its lakes and rivers are estimated at 1,547,011,792,360,000 cubic feet of water, being sufficient to envelope the entire earth with a covering of three inches in depth.

The watershed that defines the boundaries of this great basin is nowhere of great altitude: so low, indeed, is it in some places, that the waters falling into the Mississippi frequently interlock with those of the St. Lawrence basin, and the same remark is applicable to those falling into Hudson's Bay and the Atlantic ocean. In other cases short portages intervene, but oppose no substantial barrier to commercial intercourse.

On comparing the St. Lawrence with the Mississippi we find no correspondence in their respective aspects. The St. Lawrence is as remarkable for its uniformity throughout the year in the diurnal and monthly expenditure of its waters, as the Mississippi is for its continual change. A rise of three feet is a more remarkable phenomenon in the former than a rise of 30 feet in the latter. The two rivers differ widely also in numerous other particulars. The waters of the Mississippi are turbid—those of the St. Lawrence and its lakes are highly transparent. In the course of the Mississippi few lakes or enlargements occur, its banks are low, much of the surface within its basin consists of open grassy plains, and before it disembogues it divides into numerous channels. The St. Lawrence, on the contrary, consists in great part of a chain of vast lakes; as its bed enlarges, it has shelving or precipitous banks, generally covered with primeval forests; and instead of a delta, it forms at its mouth a large estuary.

THE MISSISSIPPI VALLEY OR BASIN.—We have already seen that no considerable rivers run into the lakes of the St. Lawrence; and this may prepare us for the fact, which is obvious on inspecting the map, that many of the streams which empty into the Mississippi rise very near to the lakes. Take for example the Ohio, which rises within five miles of Lake Erie, and there are many similar cases. It is a remarkable fact, that no mountains or grounds of considerable elevation, divide the tributaries of the lakes from those of the Mississippi Valley. On the contrary, the waters of Lake Michigan are so nearly on a level with the Des Plaines, (a continuation of the Illinois,) which flows into the Mississippi, that in seasons of great flood their waters not only mingle, but boats have been known to pass from the one into the other. The Valley of the Mississippi embraces all that part of the United States lying between the Alleghany or Appalachian Mountains, and the Chippewayan or Rocky Mountains; the waters of which are discharged through the mouths of the Mississippi into the Gulf of Mexico.

This great central valley may be divided into four parts. First, the portion between the lakes and the Alleghany Mountains; this is traversed by the Ohio, and its numerous confluents. Second, the portion between the lakes and the Missouri; this is traversed by the Mississippi proper. Third, the portion occupied by the Missouri itself, including the course of the River Platte. Fourth, the Valley of the Lower Mississippi with the Arkansas and Red rivers.

THE VALLEY OF THE OHIO.—The Ohio Valley is subdivided by the river into two unequal sections, leaving on the right or north-west side 80,000, and on the left or south-east side, 116,000 square miles. The Ohio river flows in a deep ravine, which forms a common recipient for the waters drained from both slopes. The length of the ravine, in a direct line from Pittsburg to the Mississippi, is 540 miles, but by following the serpentine course of the Ohio, is a distance of 948 miles. "The hills are generally found near the rivers or larger creeks, and parallel to them on each side, having between them the alluvial valley through which the stream meanders, usually near the middle, but sometimes washing the foot of either hill. Perhaps the best idea of the topography of this region may be obtained, by conceiving it to be one vast elevated plain, near the centre of which the streams rise, and in their course wearing down a bed or valley, whose depth is in proportion to their size or the solidity of the earth over which they flow. So that our hills, with some few exceptions, are nothing more or less than cliffs or banks made by the action of the streams, and although these cliffs or banks on the rivers or large creeks approach the size of mountains, yet their tops are generally level like the remains of an ancient plain."* The tributaries of the Ohio which flow from the Alleghany Mountains, are from their sources nearly to their mouths mountain torrents, and have their courses generally in deep channels, and often through deep chasms with perpendicular banks of limestone; those flowing from the north-west rise in the table-land forming the dividing ridge between the waters of the St. Lawrence and the Mississippi, with a slight current, but increase in their velocity until they unite with the Ohio. In its natural state, the valley of the Ohio was for the most part covered with a dense forest, but the central plain presents an exception. As far east as the sources of the Muskingum commence open savannahs, covered with grass and devoid of timber. Like the plain itself, those savannahs expand to the westward and open into immense natural meadows, known under the denomination of prairies. The Ohio, from Pittsburg to the Mississippi, a course of nine hundred and forty-eight miles, falls only about 400 feet, or about five inches in a mile. This river and its principal branch, the Alleghany, are in a striking manner gentle as respects currents; and from Olean, in the state of New York, to the Mississippi, over a distance of 1,160 miles, following the streams, at a moderately high flood, it meets (excepting the rapids at Louisville) with not a single serious natural impediment. The Monongahela, more impetuous, is yet

* Bourne.

navigable far into Virginia. On the north-west side of the valley the rivers are extremely rapid. Rising on a table-land from 300 to 400 feet above their mouths, and in no instance having a direct course of 300 miles, the streams, though falling gradually, are almost torrents. The Big Beaver, Muskingum, and Hockhocking, have direct falls; but the Sciota, Miami, and Wabash, though rapid, have no falls that seriously impede navigation.

The Valley of the Upper Mississippi.—The Mississippi rises in lat. 47° 10′, N., lon. 95° 54′, W., surrounded by an immense marshy plain, indented with small lakes abounding with fish and wild rice, and elevated 1,500 feet above the Gulf of Mexico. It is a circumstance peculiar to this river, that the physiognomy of nature around its head bears so strong resemblance to that of its estuary. A difference of 19 degrees of latitude precludes much similarity in vegetable or stationary animal production. "But," says Mr. Schoolcraft, who visited the sources in the month of July, "the migratory water-fowl found there at that time of the year, are very nearly the same which flock in countless millions over the Delta in December, January, February, and March. It is also deserving of remark, that its sources lie in a region of almost continual winter, while it enters the ocean under the latitude of perpetual verdure." On a view of the particular valley of the Mississippi, its general sameness first strikes the eye. No chains or groups of mountains rise to vary the scene. Over so wide a space as 180,000 square miles some solitary elevations exist, which, for want of contrast, are dignified by the name of mountains; but few continuous tracts of equal extent afford so little diversity of surface.

The upper part of the Mississippi is traversed by numerous falls and rapids of inconsiderable extent, until, after a meandering course of 420 miles, it precipitates its waters down the Falls of St. Anthony, 16½ feet perpendicular; and nine miles below receives its largest confluent, the St. Peter's, which rises among the sacred red-pipestone quarries of the Indians. The Mississippi, from the St. Peter's to some distance below Fever river, flows in small streams, (with the exception of Lake Pepin, an expansion of 20 miles in length and 5 in width,) curling among a multitude of islands, which in the summer season are clothed with grass, flowers, and forest trees; and so thickly covered, that it is said there are but three places between Prairie du Chien and St. Peter's river, a distance of 220 miles, where you can see across the river. The bluffs which bound the river are delightful to the eye, running frequently in high and continuous ridges, then divided by valleys and streams entering the river; and are covered to the summit with the same splendid verdure as the islands.

The Mississippi, after a distance of 990 miles from its source, and receiving in its course from the east the Chippewa, Wisconsin, Rock, and Illinois rivers, and many smaller streams; and from the west, the St. Peter's, Upper Iowa, Turkey, Makoqueta, Wapsipinecon, Iowa, Des Moine, and Salt rivers, and many others of less note, unites and mingles its bright waters with the dark Missouri.

THE VALLEY OF THE MISSOURI.—The Missouri rises in the Chippewayan or Rocky Mountains. As viewed from the course of this river, the mountains rise abruptly out of the plains, which lie extended at their base, and tower in peaks of great height, which render them visible at an immense distance. They consist of ridges, knobs, and peaks, variously disposed, among which are interspersed many broad and fertile valleys. The more elevated parts are covered with perpetual snow, which give them at a distance a most brilliant appearance. They are covered with a scattering growth of scrubby pine, oak, cedar, and furze. The Missouri rises far within the bosom of the mountains, and is divided by a single ridge from the waters of the Columbia, which flow into the Pacific Ocean. In its early course it flows through small but beautiful and fertile valleys, deeply embosomed amidst the surrounding heights, and forms a variety of islands in its progress, till at length it issues from these verdant recesses by a rocky pass, which has not unaptly been called the Gates of the Rocky Mountains.

* "For five and three quarter miles these rocks rise on both sides of the river, perpendicularly from the water's edge, to the height of nearly 1,200 feet. The river (three hundred and fifty yards in width) seems to have forced its channel through this solid mass; but so reluctantly has it given way, that, during the whole distance, the water is very deep, even at the edges, and for the first three miles there is not a spot, except one of a few yards, in which a man could stand between the waters and the towering perpendicular of the mountains. The convulsion of the passage must have been terrible, since at its outlet there are vast columns of rock torn from the mountains, which are strewed on both sides of the river, the trophies, as it were, of the victory. This extraordinary range of rocks is called the 'Gates of the Rocky Mountains.' At the junction of the Yellow Stone and the Missouri, the river by either branch has flowed more than a thousand miles. A few miles below the influx of the Yellow Stone, the Missouri has reached its utmost northern bend, in N. lat. 48° 20′; and curves, by a regular sweep of 200 miles, to the Mandan villages. The Platte and Kansas are two great confluents of the Missouri, rising in the same mountains, and flowing eastwardly, the former 700, and the latter 600 miles. The Platte derives its name from the circumstance of its being broad and shoal; its average width being about 1,200 yards, exclusive of the islands it embosoms, with a rapid current, and is fordable almost every-

* Lewis and Clark.

where. The character of the Kansas is nearly similar, being navigable only in high freshets, and then not exceeding 200 miles from its mouth. Grand and Chariton on the north, and Osage and Gasconade on the south, (navigable streams,) are tributaries of the Missouri. After a direct course of 1,870 miles, and a meandering one of 3,000, the Missouri unites with the Mississippi. The valley of the Missouri occupies an area of 523,000 square miles. Three remarkable features exist in it—first, the turbid character of its waters; second, the very unequal volumes of the right and left confluents; and third, the immense excess of the open prairies over the river lines of the forest. In the direction of the western rivers, the inclined plane of the Missouri extends 800 miles from the Chippewayan mountains, and rather more than that distance from south to north, from the southern branches of the Kansas to the extreme heads of the northern confluents of the valley. * "Ascending from the lower verge of this widely-extended plain, wood becomes more and more scarce, until one naked surface spreads on all sides. Even the ridges and chains of the mountains partake of these traits of desolation. The traveller in those parts, who has read the descriptions of Central Asia by Tooke or Pallas, will feel, on the higher branches of the Missouri, a resemblance at once striking and appalling. He will regret how much of the earth's surface is doomed to irremediable silence, and if near the Chippewayan heights in winter, he will acknowledge that the utmost intensity of frost in Siberia and Mongolia has its full counterpart in North America, on similar, if not on lower latitudes." "But of all the characteristics which distinguish the Missouri and its confluents, the few direct falls, or even rapids, is certainly the most remarkable. Between Dearborne's and Maria's rivers, the stream leaves the Chippewayan range by rolling over ledges of rocks for a distance of 18 miles, after which this overwhelming mass of water, though everywhere flowing with great rapidity, nowhere swells into a lake, or rolls over a single cataract, in a distance of at least 3,500 miles, to the Gulf of Mexico. If, therefore, the Amazon is excepted, the Missouri and its continuation, the Mississippi, afford the most extended, uninterrupted line of river navigation which has ever been discovered."

The Valley of the Lower Mississippi.—After being joined by the Missouri, the Mississippi makes a direct course of 820, or following its meanderings, 1,265 miles, to the Gulf of Mexico. In no circumstance is the physical geography of the United States more remarkable than in the extreme inequality of the two opposing planes, down which are poured the confluents of the Mississippi, below the influx of the Ohio. The western inclined plane, falling from the Rocky Mountains, sweeps over upwards of 800 miles; while the eastern, sloping from the Appa-

* Darby.

lachian, has not a mean width of 100 miles. The rivers which drain the two slopes are, in respective length, proportionate to the extent of their planes of descent. Although Red river exceeds a comparative course of 800 miles, the Arkansas of 1,000, and White river of 400, the longest stream from the opposite slope falls short of 200 miles. The alluvian brought down by such volumes of water as those of White, Arkansas, and Red rivers, explains satisfactorily the reason why the Mississippi infringes so often on the eastern, and nowhere below the Ohio touches the western bluffs. The lower valley of the Mississippi is the most variegated section of the United States. * "Every form of landscape, every trait of natural physiognomy, and an exhaustless quantity, with an illimitable specific diversity of vegetable and metallic productions, are found upon this extensive region. It is flanked on the east by a dense forest, and on the west by the naked ridges and spires of the Chippewayan mountains; while the deep entangled woods of the Mississippi stand in striking relief against the expansive prairies of the Arkansas and Red rivers."

INUNDATIONS OF THE MISSISSIPPI.—The spring floods to which the Mississippi is subject, are remarkable for their long and steady continuance; a circumstance highly favorable to inland navigation. It is obvious, on a glance at the different regions from whence the waters are drawn, that the rivers must be high at different periods of the year. It is evident, also, that in the breaking up of winter, the water in the same valley is drawn from its sources gradually; when, as in the case of the Mississippi, the river flows from the poles towards the equator. Similar remarks apply to the Ohio and the Arkansas; so that the duration of the flood season is thus lengthened, while the quantity of water in a given time is moderated. Generally, the Red river flows out in February, or early in March. The great flood from the Arkansas, the Ohio, and the Upper Mississippi, commences early in March, and attains its full height in the middle of June. Abating from the latter period, it has nearly subsided by the first of August, when the retarded flow of the Missouri arrives to complete the annual inundation.

FACE OF THE COUNTRY.—The surface of the Mississippi Valley may be arranged under three natural divisions—the forest, or thickly-timbered, the barrens, and prairie country. The timber most abundant in this territory are the oak, of various species, black and white walnut, ash of the several varieties, elm, sugar-maple, honey-locust, birch, buckeye, hack-berry, linden, hickory, cotton-wood, white and yellow pine, peccan, mulberry, sycamore, box, sassafras, persimmon, with several others. The undergrowth consists principally of red-bud, paw-paw, sumach, plum, crab-apple, dog-wood, hazel, spice-bush, grape-vines,

* Darby.

green-brier, &c. The trees are very luxuriant in their growth, and are frequently found of a stupendous size.

Barrens are a species of country of a mixed character, uniting forest and prairie. They are covered with scattered oaks, rough and stinted in their appearance, interspersed with patches of hazel, brushwood, and tough grass. The appearance of this description of country led the early settlers to suppose, that the scantiness of the timber was owing to the sterility of the soil, and hence, the title thus ignorantly given, became of universal application to this extensive tract of country. It is ascertained, however, that these "barrens" have as productive a soil as can be found in the Western States—healthy, more rolling than the prairies, and abounding with that important requisite, good springs. The fire passes over these "barrens" in the fall, but owing to the insufficiency of the fuel, is not able to destroy entirely the timber. The farmer may settle, without hesitation, on any part of this land, where he can find timber enough for his present wants, for the soil is better adapted to all the purposes of farming and changes of the seasons, than the deeper and richer mould of the prairies.

The next, and far most extensive surface, is the "openings," the rich level, or rolling prairies, interspersed with belts and points of timber, and the vast sterile prairies of the Far West.

And first, the "oak openings," so termed from their distinctive feature of the varieties of oak which are scattered over them, interspersed at times with pine, black-walnut, and other forest trees, which spring from a rich vegetable soil. The surface is ordinarily dry and rolling, with trees of a moderate growth. Among the "oak openings" are found some of the most lovely landscapes of the West; and for miles and miles a varied scenery of natural growth, with all the diversity of gently swelling hill and dale—here, trees grouped or standing single; and there, arranged in long avenues, as though planted with human hands, with slips of open meadow between. Sometimes the "openings" are dotted with numerous clear lakes, and form scenes of enchanting loveliness. They are fed by subterraneous springs, or the rains; and few having any apparent outlet, lose their surplus waters by evaporation. Michigan and Illinois abound with these oak openings. The rich "rolling prairie" forms the second division, which presents other features, and in a great degree another vegetation. These prairies abound with the thickest and most luxuriant belts of forest, or, as they are termed, "timbers," scattered over the open face of the country, in bands or patches of every possible form and size, generally following the meanders of the water-courses, sometimes at short distances, at other times miles and miles apart. They present wide and slightly undulating tracts of the rankest herbage and flowers, many ridges and hollows filled with purple thistles, and ponds filled with aquatic plants. In Missouri they occupy the higher portions of the country; the descent to the wooded "bottoms" being invariably over steep and stony declivities. The depth and richness of the soil on these lands are almost incredible, and the edges of the timbered strips are the favorite haunt of the emigrant settler and backwoodsman, in quest of game. Over these rolling "prairies" the fire commonly passes in the autumn, and to this cause is attributed their want of trees; as, whenever a few years elapse without the fire touching a district, the thick-sown seeds of the slumbering forest, with which the rich vegetable mould is laden, spring up from the green sod of the prairies. The surface is first covered with brushwood, composed of sumach, hazel, wild-cherry, and oak; and if the conflagrations be kept out, other forest trees follow. The third division is the vast boundless prairies of the "Far West," unbroken, save by the forest, rising on the alluvian of some water-course below their level, or by the skirts of knotted and harsh oak-wood, of thick and stinted growth. The prairies occupy the highest part of the table-land, towards the sources of the great rivers and their tributaries. They abound with abrupt and peculiarly shaped flinty hills, swelling up from the general level; great salt plains, and occasionally with isolated rocks rising from the surface, with perpendicular sides, as though cut by the hand of man, standing alone in the midst of these prairies, a wonder to the Indian and the trapper. They are seldom perfectly level. As you advance, one immense sea of grass swells to the horizon after another, unbroken, for miles, by rock or tree. They are the home of the bison, and the hunting-ground of the roving bands of the red men of the West.

Climate of the Mississippi Valley.— * "We may conceive four distinct climates between the sources and the outlet of the Mississippi. The first commencing at its source and terminating at Prairie du Chien, corresponds pretty accurately to the climate between Montreal and Boston, with this difference, that the amount of snow falling in the former is much less than in the latter region. The growing of gourd seed corn, which demands a higher temperature to bring it to maturity, is not pursued in this region. The Irish potato is raised in this climate in the utmost perfection. Wheat and cultivated grasses succeed well. The apple and pear-tree require fostering and southern exposure to bring fruit to perfection. The peach-tree has still more the habits and the delicacy of a southern stranger, and requires a sheltered declivity with a southern exposure, to succeed at all. Five months in the year may be said to be under the dominion of winter. For that length of time the cattle require shelter in the severe weather, and the still waters remain frozen. The second climate extends over the opposite states of Missouri and Illinois in their whole extent, or the country between 43° and 37°.

* Flint.

Cattle, though much benefited by sheltering, and often needing it, here seldom receive it. It is not so favorable for cultivated grasses as the preceding region. Gourd-seed corn is the only kind extensively planted. The winter commences with January and ends with the second week in February; the ice in the still waters after that time thaws. Wheat, the inhabitant of a variety of climates, is at home as a native in this. The persimmon and the paw-paw are found in its whole extent. It is the favored region of the apple, the pear, and the peach. Snow neither falls deep nor lies long. The Irish potato succeeds to a certain extent, but not as well as in the former climate; but this disadvantage is supplied by the sweet potato, which, though not at home in this climate, with a little care in the cultivation, flourishes. The grandeur of the vegetation, and the temperature of March and April, indicates an approach towards the southern regions.

"The third climate extends from 37° to 31°. Below 35°, in the rich alluvial soils, the apple-tree begins to fail in bringing its fruit to perfection; apples worth eating are seldom raised much below New Madrid. Below 33°, commences the proper climate for cotton, and here it is the staple article of cultivation. Festoons of long moss hang from the trees and darken the forest, and the palmetto gives to the low alluvial grounds a grand and striking verdure. The muscadine grape, strongly designating the climate, is first found here. Laurel-trees become common in the forest, retaining their foliage and their verdure through the winter. Wheat is no longer seen as an article of cultivation, but the fig-tree brings its fruit to full maturity.

"Below this limit to the gulf, is the fourth climate, the region of the sugar-cane and the orange-tree. It would be, if cultivated, the region of the olive. Snow is no longer seen to fall, except a few flakes in the coldest storms; the streams are never frozen; winter is only marked by nights of white frosts and days of northwest winds, which seldom last longer than three days in succession, and are followed by south winds and warm days.

"In such a variety of climate and exposure, in a country alternately covered in one point with the thickest forests, and in another spreading out into grassy plains, and with almost every shade of temperature, there must necessarily be generated all the forms and varieties of disease that spring simply from climate. Emigrants will always find it unsafe to select their residence near stagnant waters, and the rich and heavy timbered alluvions; yet these, from their fertility, and the ease in which they are brought into cultivation, are the points most frequently selected. The rich plains of the Sciota were the graves of the first settlers, but they have long since been brought into cultivation, and have lost their character for insalubrity. Hundreds of places in the West, which were selected as residences by the first emigrants on account of their fertility, and which were at first regarded as haunts of disease and mortality, have since become healthy. Wherever the 'bottoms' are wide, the forest deep, the surface level and sloping back from the river, and the vegetation rank—wherever the rivers overflow, and leave stagnant waters that are only carried off by evaporation—wherever there are in the 'bottoms,' ponds and lagoons to catch and retain the rains, and the overflow, it may be assumed as a general maxim that such places are unhealthy. Emigrants have scarcely ever paused long enough, or taken sufficient care in selecting their residences as a place of salubrity. A deep 'bottom,' a fertile soil, the margin of some navigable stream, are apt to be the determining elements of their choice. The forest is levelled, hundreds of trees moulder and putrefy about the cabin, the stagnate waters which, while shielded from the action of the sun by the forest, had remained comparatively innoxious, exposed now to the burning rays of the sun, and rendered more deleterious by being filled with trunks and branches of decaying trees, and all kinds of putrid vegetation, become laboratories of miasma, and generate on every side the seeds of disease. When it is known that such have been precisely the circumstances in which a great portion of the emigrants to the western country have fixed themselves, in open cabins that drink in the humid atmosphere of the night through a hundred crevices, in a new and untried climate, under a higher temperature, a new diet and regimen, and perhaps, under the depressing influence of severe labor and exposure, need we wonder that the country has acquired a character of unhealthiness. Yet, where the forest is cleared away, and the land has been for a sufficient time under cultivation, and is sufficiently remote from stagnant water, it generally may be considered as healthy as any other country. It is a very trite, but a true and important remark, that in proportion as the country becomes opened, cultivated, and peopled—in proportion as the redundance and rankness of natural vegetation is replaced by that of cultivation, the country becomes more healthy."

Dr. Drake remarks—"The diseases of this portion of the great valley are few, and prevail chiefly in summer and autumn. They are the offspring of the combined action of intense heat and marsh exhalation. Those who migrate from a colder climate to the southern Mississippi states, should observe the following directions: 1st. To arrive there in autumn, instead of spring or summer. 2d. If practicable, to spend the hottest part of the first two or three years in a higher latitude. 3d. To select the healthiest situation. 4th. To live *temperately*. 5th. To preserve a regular habit. Lastly. To avoid the heat of the sun, from ten in the morning till four in the afternoon; and above all, the *night air*. By a strict attention to these rules, many would escape the diseases of the climate, who annually sink under its baneful influence."

Mr. Peck observes—"The same causes for disease exist in Ohio as in

Missouri; in Michigan as in Illinois; in Kentucky and Tennessee as in Indiana. All those states are more infested with maladies which depend on variations of temperature, than the states farther south. All have localities where intermittents and agues are found, and all possess extensive districts of country where health is enjoyed, by a large proportion of emigrants. There is some difference between a heavily-timbered and a prairie country, in favor of the latter, other circumstances being equal. Changes, favorable to continued health, are produced by the settlements and cultivation of the country. In fine, I am prepared to give my opinion, *decidedly*, in favor of this country and climate. I would not certainly be answerable for all the bad locations, the imprudence and whims of all classes of emigrants, which may operate unfavorably to health."

THE PUBLIC LANDS.—Nothing can interest the American citizen or intending settler more than the history and origin of the title of the United States to the public domain, of which the general government has the sole disposal. It is a matter of deep importance to all; and as frequent inquiries are made in relation thereto, and as there is but little if any information on the subject generally disseminated, a brief summary of its more prominent points will not be out of place in this connection.

The public lands belonging to the General Government are situated:

1st. Within the United States as defined by the treaty of 1783, which terminated the Revolutionary War; and are embraced by the states of Ohio, Indiana, Illinois, Michigan, Wisconsin, and that part of Minesota east of the Mississippi river, all of which have been formed out of the North-western Territory, as conveyed with certain reservations to the United States--by New York in 1781, Virginia in 1784, Massachusetts in 1785, and Connecticut in 1786. Also the lands within the boundaries of the states of Mississippi and Alabama, north of the thirty-first degree of north latitude, as conveyed to the United States by Georgia in 1802.

2d. Within the territories of Orleans and Louisiana, as acquired from the French Republic by the treaty of 1803, including that portion of the states of Mississippi and Alabama south of the thirty-first degree of north latitude; the whole of the states of Louisiana, Arkansas, Missouri, Iowa, and that portion of Minesota west of the Mississippi river, the Indian Territory, the district of country called Nebraska, the territory of Oregon, and the region of country north of the forty-second and south of the forty-ninth degree of north latitude, which lies between Oregon and Minesota.

3d. Within the state of Florida, as obtained from Spain by the treaty of 1819; and

4th. In New Mexico and California, as acquired from the Republic of Mexico by the treaty of 1848.

Within the limits recognized by these treaties and cessions our public lands embrace an estimated area, in round numbers, of 1, 584,000,000 of acres; of which, up to 20th Sept., 1849, 146,000,000 had been disposed of, and consequently we have remaining, *unsold*, an area of 1.438,000,000 acres. These lands, in large bodies or detached tracts, are found in the states and territories mentioned within our wide-spread Republic, now stretching from the Atlantic to the Pacific ocean, and from the British Possessions on the N., to the Gulf of Mexico and the Mexican Republic on the S.

After the eventful struggle which ended in our national independence, the establishment of a system for the disposal of the public lands attracted early attention. A committee for that purpose was appointed by the Continental Congress, consisting of Messrs. Jefferson, Williamson, Howell, Gerry, and Reas, who on the 7th May, 1784, reported an "ordinance for ascertaining the mode of locating and disposing of lands in the Western Territory, and for other purposes therein mentioned." The chairman of the committee was Thomas Jefferson, of Virginia, then a delegate in Congress.

This ordinance required the public lands to be divided into "*hun dreds*" of ten geographical miles square, and those again to be subdivided into "*lots*" of one mile square each, to be numbered from 1 to 100, commencing in the north-west corner and counting from W. to E., and from E. to W. continuously—and also that the land thus subdivided should be first offered at public sale.

This ordinance was considered, debated, and amended; and upon the 3d May, 1785, on motion of Mr. Grayson, of Virginia, seconded by Mr. Monroe, the size of the township was reduced to six miles square. It was farther discussed until the 20th of May, 1785, when it was finally passed.

Our land system thus founded has gradually grown up to its present perfection, having been modified from time to time, as the condition of the country and the wants of the people required. This system, the work of our republican fathers—so simple in its theory and practice, so certain and admirable in its results—is now operating upon the organized land districts of the United States, as found in the states of Ohio, Indiana, Illinois, Michigan, Wisconsin, Iowa, Missouri, Arkansas, Louisiana, Mississippi, Alabama, Florida, and in the newly-formed territory of Minesota.

The principles of surveying are uniform and very easy of comprehension. *Meridian lines* are established and surveyed in a line due north from some important point, generally from the junction of some important water-courses. These are intersected at right angles with a *base line*. On the meridians the "townships" are numbered north or south from the *base lines*, and on the base line "ranges" are numbered east or west of the *meridian*. There are six *principal meridians* used in the surveys of the western states and territories.

The "first" *principal meridian* is a line due north from the mouth of the Great Miami river to the old northern boundary of Ohio, with a *base line* extending due E. on the 41st degree of north latitude.

The "second" *principal meridian* is a line due north from a point on the Ohio river to the northern boundary of Indiana.

The "third" *principal meridian* is a line due north from the junction of the Ohio and Mississippi rivers to the northern boundary of Illinois. The *base line* for the second and third principal meridians commences on the Ohio at 38° 30′ N. lat., and extends due W. to the Mississippi.

The "fourth" *principal meridian* commences on the Illinois river, at a point 72 miles due north from its mouth; (here also commences its *base line*, and runs due west to the Mississippi river.) The meridian continues north (crossing and recrossing the Mississippi river) to the Wisconsin river, with an additional *base line* on the north boundary of Illinois for the surveys in Wisconsin.

The "fifth" *principal meridian* is a line beginning at the mouth of the Arkansas river, thence through the states of Arkansas and Missouri to township 54 north, where it crosses the Mississippi, recrosses into Iowa, and continues to the Mississippi river near Cassville. Its *base line* extends due west from the mouth of White river to the western boundary of Arkansas.

The "sixth" *principal meridian* is used for the state of Michigan, and begins on the south boundary of the state in a due north direction from the junction of the Maumee and Au-Glaize rivers to the Straits of Mackinaw, having a base line crossing the peninsula in a due west line from about the center of Lake St. Clair to Lake Michigan.

6	5	4	3	2	1
7	8	9	10	11	12
18	17	16*	15	14	13
19	20	21	22	23	24
30	29	28	27	26	25
31	32	33	34	35	36

When a *meridian* and *base line* have been laid out, township lines are run (at a distance of six miles) parallel to the meridian and base line. These form townships of six miles square, containing an area of 36 square miles. Each square mile is a "section," and contains 640 acres. The sections are numbered from 1 to 36, be-

* The 16th section of each township is appropriated for school purposes in all the new states.

ginning at the north-east corner of the township, as seen in the annexed diagram.

Sections are subdivided into half sections of 320 acres, (*see* diagram No. 1;) into quarter sections of 160 acres, (*see* No. 2;) and half quarter sections of 80 acres, (*see* No. 3.) Prior to the year 1820 no person could purchase less than a quarter, but in that year legal authority was given for the division and sale of the sections into eighths. And in 1832, a further accommodation to settlers, they were divided into sixteenths, or 40-acre lots, (*see* No. 4.) The following diagrams will illustrate the plan of dividing adopted in the surveys:

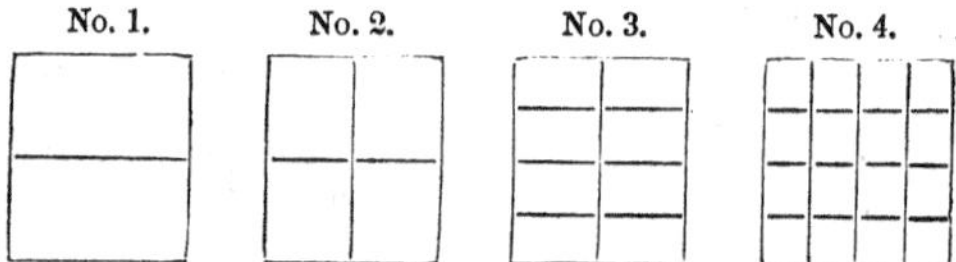

The privilege of having them thus minutely subdivided was, by act of Congress, 1846, extended to all purchasers at private sale. The corners of townships, sections, and quarter sections, are designated by monuments established by the surveyors on the field.

After the lands have been thus surveyed, they are proclaimed by the President for sale, and offered at public auction at not less than $1.25 per acre; and such as thereafter remain unsold are subject to be purchased at private sale at that rate. As only a small portion of the lands thus offered are disposed of at public sales, our own citizens, as well as emigrants from all parts of the world, have at all times an opportunity of selecting and purchasing at private sale rich and fertile tracts possessing every requisite for desirable farms.

The security of titles emanating under this system has greatly contributed to the rapid settlement of the public lands. The positions o all tracts are shown by the surveys on the ground, in strict conformity with legislative direction; so that even when the monuments, by which they are indicated, perish under the consuming influence of time, they can still be identified, and their boundaries determined with unerring accuracy.

In conveying these lands to purchasers, the brief designation of the number of the lot, or its position in the section, with the number of the section, township, and range, will as fully and certainly convey the title as could be done by the most critical detail of boundaries and labored description of courses and distances. This is fully shown by the fact, that although this system has been extended over hundreds of millions of acres, including every variety of soil and climate, occupied by people from almost every civilized portion of the world, litigation, as to boundaries, has been so inconsiderable as to place the superiority of this national system in striking contrast with those of the older states of the confederacy. Indeed, where there has been litigation, it has been mainly caused by frauds, and not by any defect in the plan of operation.

In reviewing this subject in all its details, the mind is forcibly impressed with the sagacity and foresight of the great public men who organized our institutions, and who, in this, as in all their public acts, have left imperishable monuments of profound wisdom, pure patriotism, and enlarged philanthropy.

Under this system the wilderness of the West, in less than half a century, has been transformed into fruitful farms, and filled with flourishing cities; and settlers from the original states, and from all parts of Europe, have there secured homes for their families, and rich reward for their industry.

That the benefit of education might be extended to them and their posterity, the sixteenth section in each township, or one thirty-sixth part of the public lands, has been set apart for the support of schools, besides munificent donations being from time to time made by Congress for colleges, seminaries, seats of government, county seats, and internal improvements. Indeed, our government has always exercised a prudent and patient care over the interests of settlers, and secured to them the advantages of an enlightened system of political and social existence.

In many cases persons have settled on the public lands without purchase, as "squatters," and have made improvements on their clandestine occupations. To secure such settlers from injury, Congress has passed a pre-emption law, which gives them the privilege of purchasing at a minimum price to the exclusion of all others, who previous to the passage of that act, were entitled to purchase and drive away the original improver without recompense for his labor.

The management of the public lands is vested in a Commissioner, who is subordinary to the Secretary of the Interior. The General Land-office, of which he is the head, is located in Washington City. For the convenience of purchasers, and the easier transaction of business, however, local offices are established in different places, to each of which a surveyor and receiver is attached. The following are the localities of the offices of all the land districts in the Western States:

In *Ohio.*—Chilicothe and Defiance.

In *Indiana.*—Jeffersonville, Vincennes, Indianapolis, Crawfordville, Fort Wayne, and Winamac.

In *Michigan.*—Detroit, Kalamazoo, Genesee, Ionia, and Sault St. Marie.

In *Illinois.*—Shawneetown, Kaskaskia, Edwardsville, Vandalia, Palestine, Springfield, Danville, Quincy, Dixon, and Chicago.

In *Wisconsin.*—Mineral Point, Menasha, Milwaukee, Stevens' Point, La Crosse, and Willow River.

In *Missouri.*—St. Louis, Fayette, Palmyra, Jackson, Clinton, Springfield, Plattsburg, and Milan.

In *Iowa.*—Dubuque, Fairfield, Iowa City, Fort Desmoines, Kanesville, Chariton, Northern and Missouri River.

In *Minesota.*—Stillwater and Sauk Rapids.

It is at these offices that all sales of the lands are made, and all business between the government and the settler transacted.

The following table will exhibit the area of each of the Western States in acres; the number of acres disposed of by sale, donation, grant, &c.; and the number of acres of public lands remaining at the disposal of the General Government on the 1st January, 1849.*

States.	Date of first sales.	Area.	Sold.	Donations to Schools and Universities.
		Acres.	Acres.	Acres.
Ohio	1787	25,576,960	12,490,215	713,608
Michigan	1818	35,995,520	9,071,223	1,115,348
Indiana	1807	21,637,760	15,477,629	696,397
Illinois	1814	35,459,200	15,040,145	1,024,835
Missouri	1818	43,123,200	9,726,361	1,245,219
Iowa	1838	32,584,960	2,361,022	951,224
Wisconsin	1844	34,511,360	4,567,095	1,004,728
Total		228,888,960	68,733,690	6,751,359

(Table continued.)

States.	Grants for Internal Improvements.	Other disposals.†	Remaining with General Government
	Acres.	Acres.	Acres.
Ohio	1,181,135	10,384,436	807,566
Michigan	500,000	251,245	25,057,704
Indiana	1,609,862	582,141	3,271,731
Illinois	500,000	3,895,282	14,998,938
Missouri	500,000	2,214,678	29,436,942
Iowa	825,078	79,199	28,368,437
Wisconsin	858,400	650,107	27,431,030
Total	5,974,475	18,057,088	129,372,348

The quantity of swamp land, as reported by the Surveyor-General, in each state is as follows: Ohio, 303,329 acres; Michigan, 4,544,189 acres; Indiana, 981,682 acres; Illinois, 1,833,413 acres; Missouri, 1,517,287 acres; Iowa, 33,813 acres; Wisconsin, 1,259,269 acres.

* The aggregate disposals of land for the nine months ending 1st Oct., 1849, was 3,706,296 acres.

† Including "grants to individuals and companies;" "grants for seats of government and public buildings;" "military bounties;" "reservations—Indian, and military and naval;" "private claims confirmed," &c.

DESCRIPTION

OF THE

WESTERN STATES AND TERRITORIES.

THE STATE OF OHIO.

Area 39,964 *square miles.—Population* 1,980,329.

THIS flourishing and populous state is situated between 38° 34′ and 42° N. lat., and between 80° 35′ and 84° 57′ W. long. and is bounded N. by Michigan and Lake Erie; E. by Pennsylvania and Virginia; S. by Kentucky, and W. by Indiana. The Ohio river runs along its southern and the greater part of its eastern boundary for 462 miles, separating the state from Virginia and Kentucky.

The northern part of Ohio, bordering on Lake Erie, and the interior, are generally level, and in some places marshy. In the E. and S. E. the country is much broken, often rising into rugged and abrupt elevations, but nowhere becoming mountainous. The whole state may be said to be susceptible of cultivation, and certainly it is one of the most productive and fertile in the Union. In the valleys of the Sciota and the Great and Little Miami, are found the finest portions of the country. In a state of nature, Ohio, with the exception of the central prairies, was covered with dense forests, to which the fertility of the soil gave stupendous development. The most extensive prairies are those of the central table-land. The principal rivers, besides the great and beautiful river which gives its name to the state, are the Mahoning, Beaver, Muskingum, Hockhocking, Sciota, and the Little and Great Miami, which flow south into the Ohio river; and the Maumee, Sandusky, Huron, Grand, and Ashtabula, which fall into Lake Erie, which forms the northern boundary of the state for 160 miles. The climate is one of the most healthy. Free from the extremes of heat and cold, it is peculiarly adapted to agricultural and other out-door employments, and to this fact is no doubt owing the general prosperity of the inhabitants.

Numerous remains of former and extinct races are found in various parts. These consist of tumuli or mounds, and ancient fortifications of earth, articles of earthenware, &c. To what people or time these are to be referred, is questionable; but it is evident that the race of Indians found in these territories by the first explorers, have had no connection with them: indeed, they were entirely ignorant of their origin, nor were they acquainted with their use or economy.

Ohio is extensively engaged in all the great branches of industry; but agriculture is the chief employment of the inhabitants. All the cereals, fruits, and other products of moderate climates, are cultivated; and in the rearing of live-stock, the state is pre-eminent, and for this no state has better facilities. Of hogs alone, about 600,000 are annually slaughtered, and the yearly production of wool amounts to near 11,000,000 lbs. The mineral wealth of Ohio, consisting of iron, coal, salt, &c., is immense, but as yet only partially developed, and building material is abundant. Gold is said to have been found near Lisbon. Manufactures are carried on with success, and are daily increasing in importance. The exports consist of wheat, pork, wool, and other agricultural staples. These find outlets at the lake ports and the ports on the Ohio. Internal communication is provided for by a splendid system of railroads and canals. Every element of prosperity indeed is here in active operation. The length of railroad now completed is 2,100 miles, and the length of canal nearly 900 miles.

Education is munificently provided for. There are in the state 12,279 common schools, with an average attendance of 437,000 children. The school fund owned by the state amounts to $1,566,931. There are also about 130 academies, twelve colleges, six theological seminaries, one law school, and two medical schools. The number of private schools is also very large. The state also supports an Asylum for the Insane, and a Deaf and Dumb Asylum.

The state is divided into 87 counties. The principal cities and towns are—Columbus, Cincinnati, Cleveland, Sandusky, Springfield, Portsmouth, Marietta, &c.

COLUMBUS, the capital, is situated about the middle of the state, on the E. bank of the Sciota, immediately below the junction of the Whetstone river. The streets are laid out rectangularly; and in the center of the city is a fine public square. The great national road intersects here, and is carried over the river by a bridge, which also unites the city with Franklinton. Population 17,883. CHILICOTHE, on the W. bank of the river, 60 miles south, and PORTSMOUTH, at its mouth, are places of considerable importance and population. In the neighborhood of Portsmouth is a large number of furnaces.

CINCINNATI, the "Queen city of the West," is situated on the north bank of the Ohio, near the western border of the state. It is the largest city in Ohio, and in point of population the fifth in the United States. Its public buildings are numerous, and equal to those of any city of like population. In manufactures, trade, and commerce, it is pre-eminent. Population in 1810, 2,540; in 1850, 115,438. It is connected both by canal and railroad with Lake Erie, and with the whole east and west by the noble Ohio. SPRINGFIELD, on the E. fork of Mad river, 84 miles north by railroad, is a rapidly increasing town, engaged in manufactures, and has considerable commercial connection.

The other towns on the Ohio deserving of notice are GALLIPOLIS, an improving place, and capital of Gallia county—population 1,686· COALPORT, the chief depôt of mining operations; POMEROY, a place of extensive traffic—population 1,637; MARIETTA, on the E. bank of the Muskingum, at its mouth, noted for its mills—population 3,133; STEUBENVILLE, the center of a rich and populous country—population 6,140 &c., &c.

ZANESVILLE, on the E. bank of the Muskingum, 80 miles N. of Marietta, is a manufacturing town of about 7,791 inhabitants. Anthracite coal and a clay suitable for earthenware are found in the neighborhood. The national road passing through the town, makes it a great thoroughfare, and, by the improvements in the river, navigation is opened to the Ohio, while the Ohio Canal unites it with Lake Erie and the Sciota river. COSHOCTON, NEW PHILADELPHIA, BOLIVAR, MASSILLON, and FULTON, are also on the Muskingum, N. of Zanesville. AKRON, 34 miles S. of Cleveland, and about 10 miles N. of Fulton, is an important canal center.

CLEVELAND, at the mouth of the Cuyahoga river, and the northern terminus of the Ohio Canal, is the most important of the lake ports. It is excellently situated for commerce, and has now a population of 19,000. SANDUSKY CITY, situated on the S. side of Sandusky Bay, about three miles from Lake Erie, is a point of importance. It is united with Cincinnati by railroad, and also with Mansfield and Newark. The port is continually thronged with vessels during the open season. Population 5,088. TOLEDO, near the mouth of the Maumee, and on the Wabash and Erie Canal, is the eastern terminus of the railroad to Adrian in Michigan, and possesses superior advantages as a commercial depôt. It is constantly progressing, and must eventually, with the natural and artificial means at its disposal, at no distant period become one of the most important places on the lake coast. The present population is only about 4,000. PORT CLINTON, PAINESVILLE, ASHTABULA, &c., are also places of great commercial importance, and are rapidly increasing in population.

Previous to 1788 the whole of Ohio was a wilderness. In that year a settlement was made at Marietta, and in 1789 the country was placed under a territorial government, and called the "Western Territory." This designation was applied not only to Ohio, but to all the district north-west of the Ohio to the Mississippi river, and included the states of Indiana, Michigan, Illinois, Wisconsin, and part of the territory of

Minesota. At a subsequent period it was known as the "Territory north-west of the Ohio." The ordinance by which this territory was established forbade slavery in any future state that might be formed within the district. The Indian wars in Ohio were terminated by Wayne's expedition in 1794. In 1802 this state was received into the Union. Since then no state has increased so rapidly, and it now ranks as third in population and wealth.

THE STATE OF MICHIGAN.

Area 56,243 *square miles.—Population* 397,654.

MICHIGAN lies between 41° 48′ and 47° 30′ N. lat., and between 82° 20′ and 90° 10′ W. long.: and is bounded N. by Lake Superior; E. by St. Mary's river, Lake Huron, St. Clair river, Lake St. Clair, Detroit river, and Lake Erie; S. by the states of Ohio and Indiana, and W. by Lake Michigan and the Menomonee and Montreal rivers. The state consists of two distinct peninsulas.

The "Southern Peninsula," or Michigan proper, contains an area of 39,856 square miles. The surface is generally level, but has a gradual ascent from the shores to the center of the country, where it attains an elevation of 600 or 700 feet. The coasts of Lakes Michigan and Huron have high and steep banks, and along the former are bluffs and sand hills from 100 to 300 feet elevation. The interior is mostly covered with fine forests, interspersed with prairie and openings. The country is drained by several large rivers and numerous smaller streams, which rise near the center, and pass off in an E. and W. direction. The Cheboygan and some small streams, however, flow N. into Mackinaw Strait. The larger rivers are navigable almost to their sources. Raisin and Huron rivers flow E. into Lake Erie; Rouge into Detroit river; Clinton and Black into the St. Clair; and Saginaw, formed by the union of several streams, into Saginaw Bay. But the largest rivers flow into Lake Michigan. St. Joseph's, Kalamazoo, Grand, and Maskegon rivers are all navigable by steam. Several lakes are found in the northern part of the peninsula. The quality of soil is very various: in the north there are considerable sandy tracts and marshes; but on the whole the country is not unfertile, and not much inferior to the fine lands of the South for agricultural purposes. No part of the Union is better supplied with fish, game, and wild fowl, and the climate is remarkably mild, being tempered by the large bodies of water by which it is almost surrounded.

The "Northern Peninsula," between lakes Michigan and Superior, occupies 16,387 square miles. Portions of it are the mere development of sublime scenery. Mountains and plains, lakes, rivers, and forests spread over it with a boldness of outline which may be said to constitute almost a peculiar type in North American geography. This division embraces the "mineral district" of Michigan. Much of it falls under the influence of causes which render it of little value in an agricultural point of view. The northern shores of lakes Michigan and Huron are exclusively limestone, and abound in gypsum and saline springs. The interior abounds in small lakes, and enjoys a singular advantage of intercommunication by its streams and portages. The length of coast navigation is about 750 miles, and in this distance are embraced several large bays and excellent harbors. About 40 large, and some 60 small streams, discharge their waters into the lakes constituting portions of its boundary. The whole peninsula is eminently distinguished for the value and diversity of its minerals. Copper exists in vast beds in the neighborhood of Lake Superior, and is frequently found in its native state. In some of the river beds large boulders of this mineral are frequently met with. Iron of a very superior quality is also found; and recent surveys have developed the fact that it exists in an almost pure state, and in larger bodies than even in the state of Missouri. The copper mines are now being worked by a number of Eastern capitalists, and large amounts of ore and reduced metal are finding their way into the markets.

The favorable situation of Michigan, having immediate access to four of the great American lakes; its fine soil and climate; its mineral resources and other advantages, must eventually make it one of the most prosperous of the Western states. Its industry is as yet only in its infancy, and its capabilities only partially known. The farmers raise almost every staple of temperate climates, and are rich in live-stock. The chief cereal crops consist of wheat, oats, and Indian corn. Barley, rye, and buckwheat, are raised in small quantities. Maple sugar is a never-failing crop. The products of both wild and domestic animals are large. Manufactures are progressing, but as yet are confined chiefly to articles of immediate necessity. Michigan is perhaps better situated for commerce than any other inland state. It is now accessible from New York and New Orleans wholly by water, and with those places maintains considerable traffic. Canada overlooks its eastern shores, and in several places is only separated by narrow straits. With regard to its inland trade, every facility is enjoyed that navigable rivers and excellent roads can afford. Already the exports amount to an important sum. Flour, wheat, corn, pork, beef, fish, wool, leather, &c., constitute its chief exports. Taxable property in the state, real and personal, amounts to $29,908,769. The railroads in Michigan have a total length of 474 miles, the main lines running across the southern part of the lower peninsula.

The University, founded in 1837, is located at Ann Arbor, and has three departments: viz., for literature and the sciences, law, and medicine. It is supported by a fund arising from lands appropriated to its use by Congress, and is governed by a Board of Regents. No charge is made for tuition. Provision is made by law for 26 professorships, and also for the establishment of departments for female education, for the education of teachers, and for agricultural science; but the institution as now organized consists only of seven professors, and the three departments as above named. Primary schools are established throughout the state, and governed by local boards, supported by taxes and a general school-fund. There are 435 townships in the state, in 270 of which school libraries are supported, and provision is also made for district libraries. The number of school districts in the state is 2,869, and the number of scholars 97,658. The amount expended annually is about $140,000. Instruction is under the general supervision of a superintendent. The Catholic college of St. Philip's, near Detroit, was founded in 1839, and in 1849 had four professors and about 37 students. A state normal school was established at Ypsilanti in 1849.

Michigan is divided into 64 counties. The principal cities and towns are Lansing, Detroit, Pontiac, Monroe, Ann Arbor, Ypsilanti, Tecumseh, Adrian, Marshall, Kalamazoo, Niles, New Buffalo, all in the southern portion of the state; Grand Rapids and Maskegon, on the rivers of the same name; Saginaw, on Saginaw river; Port Huron, at the N. entrance of St. Clair river, &c.

Lansing, the capital, is situated in Ingham county, on Grand river, 117 miles from Detroit, and has been the seat of government since Dec. 1847. It is centrally situated in reference to the settlements. Though but a few years have elapsed since the place was a wilderness, it now contains upwards of 400 houses and several large hotels. The State House is a spacious and handsome building, in the center of an enclosure overlooking the town, and on an elevation of about 50 feet above the river. Several saw and flouring mills, propelled both by steam and water power, have been erected, and there seems to be every prospect of its becoming a flourishing place. Pop. 1,229. A stage communication is maintained to Jackson, on the Central Railroad.

Detroit, the former capital, and the largest and most flourishing town in Michigan, is well situated for trade on the W. side of Detroit river, seven miles S. of Lake St. Clair, and 18 N. of Lake Erie. It stands on an elevated site, about 30 feet above the water. It is regularly laid out, and has many excellent public buildings and private residences. It enjoys great facilities for an extensive commerce, and few cities have better prospects for future eminence. Pop. 34,436. The Central Railroad extends hence to New Buffalo, 221 miles, and another to Pontiac, 25 miles. Detroit was formerly a military post of the French, and a great depôt of the fur-traders.

PONTIAC, 25 miles N. W. from Detroit, on the N. bank of Clinton river, contains the county buildings of Oakland, and is a flourishing inland town, containing several manufactures. Population 2,819. It is connected with Detroit by railroad. SHELBY and MT. CLEMENS, on the same river, to the E. of Pontiac, are considerable villages. ST. CLAIR and PORT HURON, on St. Clair river, occupy excellent commercial sites, and with the progress of settlement must become important. MONROE, 39 miles S. of Detroit, is well situated, both for manufactures and commerce, at the lower falls of Raisin river, and is accessible for the largest vessels from Lake Erie. Population 3,646. Here commences the Southern Railroad. ADRIAN and TECUMSEH, also on the Raisin, are populous villages, the former of which is a station on the Southern Railroad. HILLSDALE, on same road, has 1,067 inhabitants· YPSILANTI, the seat of the State Normal School, and ANN ARBOR, the seat of Michigan University, are towns on the S. bank of Huron river, and on the line of the Central Railroad. The population of each is about 4,870. DEXTER, JACKSON, and MARSHALL are towns on the same railroad. Marshall, which is situated on the N. bank of Kalamazoo river, is an important place, with a population of about 2,823. KALAMAZOO, on the S. bank, has great commercial advantages, the river being navigable to the lake. It has long been an important point of travel, and has especially increased in prosperity since the completion of the Central Railroad. A large trade centers here from the neighboring country. Population 2,507. NILES, on the E. side of St. Joseph's river, at the head of steam navigation, is an important place on the Central Railroad. Population 2170. NEW BUFFALO, opposite Chicago, on Lake Michigan, is the W. terminus of the Central Railroad, and distant from Detroit 221 miles. It has much of the busy aspect of its great prototype of the east. ST. JOSEPH'S, at the mouth of the river of the same name, has a good location for commerce, but hitherto has not realized the expectations of its founders.

GRAND RAPIDS is situated on the S. E. side of Grand river, at the rapids, which have a fall of 15 feet in a mile, and afford immense water-power. A large number of splendid saw and flouring mills have been erected here. The village contains the public offices of Kent county, and has a population of about 3,200. A canal round the rapids would secure navigation to steamboats many miles further up the river. It was founded in 1833, and promises to become one of the most important places in the state. MASKEGON, on the S. bank of the river of the same name, is also a large village, and well located for commerce. It is the natural outlet of an extensive back-country. Pop 404.

SAGINAW, on the W. bank of Saginaw river, 23 miles from its mouth, stands on an elevated site, and contains several substantial public buildings. It has long been an important village, and has considerable commerce. It is the chief outlet for the extensive country watered by the numerous tributaries of the Saginaw. Pop 917.

MACKINAW, on Mackinaw Island, which forms a part of the N. E. bank of the strait of Mackinaw, is a village of some 800 inhabitants. It is an important military station, occupied by the U. S. forces. The fortifications are built on an eminence, 160 feet above the surface of the lake. The Indians resort to this station to receive from government their annuities, and are here met by the traders. Steamboats call here on their passages through the strait.

Few villages exist in the northern peninsula. Those occupied by the miners are only of a temporary nature. SAULT ST. MARIE, however, is an exception. This village, 90 miles N. W. from Mackinaw, is situated near the rapids of St. Mary's river, between lakes Superior and Huron, and at the head of steam navigation. It is proposed to connect the two lakes by a canal round the falls, and thus secure a continuous navigation between the lakes, and form an outlet for the vast resources of the upper lake country.

The first permanent settlement within the bounds of Michigan was made by the French at Detroit in 1670; but at the peace of Paris in 1763, the country was transferred to England, and at the close of the Revolutionary war reverted to the United States. In 1805 it was erected by Congress into a separate territorial government. During the last war with England it fell into the hands of the enemy through the cowardice of Gen. Hull, but was retaken by Gen. Harrison in the following year On 13th of June, 1836, it was admitted as a state of the Union. Arkansas was admitted on the same day as a slave state.

THE STATE OF INDIANA.

Area 33,809 *square miles.—Population* 988,416.

INDIANA lies between 37° 45′ and 41° 52′ N. lat., and between 84° 42′ and 88° 12′ W. long.: and is bounded N. by Lake Michigan and the state of the same name; E. by Ohio; S. E. and S. by the Ohio river, and W. by the Wabash river and Illinois.

The physical aspect of this state is generally similar to that of Ohio. In no part is it mountainous; but that portion bordering on the Ohio river contains much broken and hilly land. The interior is undulating, and in many parts clothed with timber. The river bottoms are always rich and fertile. On the shores of Lake Michigan are extensive sand-hills, and along the course of the Kankakee river swamps and marshes. The Ohio meanders along the entire southern boundary. The E. and W. forks of the White river and the Wabash drain the whole western and central portion of the state. The Wabash is navigable for steamboats to Logansport, and the head waters of this river interlace with those of the St. Joseph's and Maumee. It falls into the Ohio in the S. W. corner of the state, and forms the western border for 160 miles. The climate is comparatively mild, and highly favorable for agriculture; and with few local exceptions, the whole country is remarkably healthy.

Iron ore and bituminous coal are abundant, and salt is manufactured in several counties. Few persons, however, are employed in mining. Agriculture engrosses almost universal attention. Wheat, oats, and Indian corn are the great cereal staples, and are largely exported, as are also wool and pork. Tobacco is also produced. Indiana is progressing in manufactures, and in this branch a large capital is already employed. The commerce of the state is chiefly carried on through the Ohio; and to the ports on that river most of the exports are brought by the Wabash, and the several internal improvements. Michigan City is the only port of consequence on Lake Erie. The length of completed railroad in the state is 1,208 m., and of canal 420 miles.

The school fund amounts to $4,988,988, but in this are included as a total, the estimated value of school lands unsold. The number of academies is about 80, and of common schools 2,000. There are also six colleges in the state, one theological seminary, one law school, and one medical school. About 90,000 students and scholars attend these institutions.

Indiana is divided into 90 counties. The chief cities and towns are—Indianapolis, Evansville, Jeffersonville, Madison, Lawrenceburg, Covington, Logansport, Michigan City, &c.

Indianapolis, the capital, is situated on the E. bank of the West Fork of White river, and at the head of steam navigation. An elegant bridge is thrown over the river, over which passes the great national road. The State House is one of the most splendid buildings in the West, and is modelled after the Parthenon at Athens. The city contains also several handsome churches and school-houses. It was laid out in 1821, and now has a population of 9,000. A railroad extends hence to Madison, on the Ohio.

Lawrenceburg, on the Ohio, is a place of importance, at the south terminus of the Whitewater Canal, but is liable to inundation. It is a great depot for the rich produce of the Miami and Whitewater valleys, and will ultimately become a large city. Population 4.500. Vevay was settled by a Swiss colony in 1804, and is the seat of Switzerland county. It has a fine location, and is prettily laid out, being surrounded by vineyards. The lands in the neighborhood, indeed, were granted by Congress, with the stipulation to make vine culture a prominent part of the agriculture of the colonists. Population 2,000. MADISON derives importance from being the southern terminus of the railroad, 86 miles long, to the capital. It has great facilities for both manufactures and commerce. Population 12,200. JEFFERSONVILLE, opposite Louisville, is the site of the State Prison. Population 3,800. NEW ALBANY is a large and flourishing place, and carries on some manufactures. Ship-building is one of its chief businesses. A railroad extends hence to Chicago *via* Salem, Lafayette, and Michigan City, at the latter place connecting with the Michigan Central R. R. Population 8,181. ROME and ROCKPORT are lower down the Ohio. EVANSVILLE has an extensive trade with the interior. It is connected by a canal with Lake Erie, 458 miles N. N. E. Several manufactures are carried on in the town. Population 8,000. MT. VERNON, 22 miles W., is the capital of Posey county, and a flourishing village.

VINCENNES, on the Wabash, 150 miles from its mouth, is the oldest city in the state, having been settled by the French in 1702. The inhabitants are chiefly descendants of the old colonists, and still retain much of their national vivacity and politeness. It was formerly the state capital. Population 2,800. NEW HARMONY, 50 miles S. of Vincennes, was settled in 1816 by a colony of German enthusiasts, styled "Harmonists," under the spiritual charge of George Rapp. These religionists ultimately settled on Beaver Creek, Pa., and their lands were purchased by Robert Owen, the Scottish Socialist, who here attempted to test the operation of his "new-light" principles on a large scale. About 1,000 persons congregated here under his system, but the experiment was soon abandoned, and the place is now a mere village. TERRE HAUTE, on the Ohio and Erie Canal, about 100 miles N. of Vincennes, and LOGANSPORT, at the head of steam navigation on the Wabash, are important places. LAFAYETTE, WILLIAMSPORT, COVINGTON, and NEWPORT, are also flourishing towns on the Wabash. Opposite Lafayette was fought the famous battle of Tippecanoe.

MICHIGAN CITY is the only port in Indiana on the lake. There are some considerable towns and villages in the eastern portion of the state, but none of large population, or of much consequence to the traveller.

The early history of Indiana is obscure. The first settlement was made at Vincennes by French soldiers from Canada in 1702. In 1763 the territory was ceded to the British, and afterwards formed a part of the Western Territory. Indian wars desolated the country until 1797, and in 1811-12, the Indians, incited by the British, again commenced hostilities. The battle of Tippecanoe compelled them to sue for peace. In

1816, Indiana was admitted into the Union; and since that period has been rapidly filling up with a hardy and vigorous immigration, and now ranks fifth in point of population.

THE STATE OF ILLINOIS.

Area 55,405 *square miles.—Population* 851,470.

Illinois, so noted for the extent of its prairies, is situated between 37° and 42° 30′ N. lat., and between 87° 49′ and 91° 30′ W. long.: and is bounded N. by Wisconsin; E. by Lake Michigan and Indiana; S. E. and S. by the Ohio river, which separates it from Kentucky, and W. by the Mississippi, which flows from the N. southward, between it and Iowa and Missouri.

The surface is generally level: the southern and northern parts of the state are somewhat hilly and broken, but nowhere mountainous. That portion S. of a line from the mouth of the Wabash to the mouth of the Kaskaskia river, is mostly covered with timber: thence N. prairie predominates. A range of bluffs commences on the margin of the Mississippi, (a short distance above the mouth of the Ohio,) and extend N. of the Des Moines rapids, sometimes rising abruptly from the water's edge, but most generally at a few miles distant, having between the bluffs and river a strip of alluvial formation of the most exhaustless fertility. Probably two-thirds of the state is prairie land. The soil throughout is excellent,—rich, deep, and productive, being watered by an abundance of pure springs, and well adapted for all kinds of grain, and other agricultural staples of temperate climes. The great lead region in this state is in the N. W. portion, and the mines in the neighborhood of Galena are perhaps the richest in the world. Copper and iron ores also exist, and coal is found in almost every county, while salt-springs abound in the southern counties. The Mississippi, Ohio, and Wabash rivers form more than two-thirds of the boundary of the state. The Big-Muddy, Kaskaskia, Illinois, and Rock rivers, and many smaller streams, empty themselves into the Mississippi. Chicago river empties into Lake Michigan; the Vermillion, Embarras, and Little Wabash into the Wabash river, which, and some few others, empty into the Ohio. The state is everywhere well watered. The climate is excellent, and in the south is sufficiently mild for the cultivation of cotton, while peaches come to maturity everywhere. Except on the river bottoms, and in the neighborhood of swamps, the country is healthy, and free from endemic diseases.

The productive industry of Illinois is chiefly employed in agriculture. The cereal staples are wheat, oats, and Indian corn. Tobacco, hemp, and flax are also raised The manufactures are comparatively of small importance. Mining, however, is briskly carried on, and large quantities of lead, copper, iron, and bituminous coal are annually produced. The lead region extends from Galena beyond the limits of the state north and west, and is supposed to occupy a district 200 miles long and 60 broad. Mining operations have been carried on for 30 years. Illinois has but little direct foreign commerce, but supplies no inconsiderable amount of that carried on with other states; and since the completion of the Illinois Canal a large export business has been done *via* the lakes. The Mississippi river, however, will ever be the great outlet for the productions of the interior. Many of the rivers are navigable, and with the already completed internal improvements, afford great facilities for the transportation of goods and merchandise. Illinois has projected a splendid system of railroads, but only 1,312 miles are completed. The canal from the lake to the Illinois river, however, is finished, and answers perfectly every anticipation of its projectors.

Illinois has four colleges, a theological seminary, and a medical school. There are also about 60 academies and grammar schools in the state, which educate about 3,500 students; and 3,955 common schools, at which 51,447 children are taught for various terms during the year. The whole number of persons under 20 years of age was in 1852, 361,954. The school fund amounts to $3,373,096 There is a Deaf and Dumb Asylum at Springfield, which, in Jan. 1853, had 109 pupils.

The state is divided into 99 counties. The following are among the principal cities and towns—Springfield, Chicago, Galena, Rock Island, Nauvoo, Quincy, Kaskaskia, Alton, Cairo, Shawneetown, &c

Springfield, the capital, is situated on the border of a beautiful plain, 4 miles S. of the Sangamon river, and very near the center of the state. In 1823 it contained about 30 families, living in small log cabins. It now has several fine public buildings, including the capitol, an elegant edifice of hewn stone, and a population of 5,000. The surrounding country is one of the richest prairie districts in the state.

Chicago is situated on the S. W. shore of Lake Michigan, and is the most commercial city of Illinois. It is built on a level prairie, elevated somewhat above the lake surface, and lies on both sides of Chicago river, about a mile above its entrance in the lake. By the construction of piers, an artificial harbor has been made at the mouth of the river. The city has sprung up rapidly. In 1830 it was a mere trading post; it now contains about 29,963 inhabitants, and is one of the largest grain depôts in the Union. Its commerce is immense, and in the aggregate employs about 60,000 tons of shipping, one half steamers and propellers. The lumber trade is also becoming very profitable. This trade is chiefly carried on with Buffalo. Chicago is connected with the western rivers by a sloop canal, one of the most magnificent works ever undertaken. It is connected with the Mississippi at several points by railroad.

GALENA, in the heart of the lead regions, is situated on Fever river, 7 miles from the Mississippi, and derives all its importance from the mining carried on in the vicinity. Population 7,000. A railroad connects it with Chicago, and also with Cairo.

ROCK ISLAND, near the mouth of Rock river, is an island about 4 miles long and 2 broad. It is the site of Fort Armstrong, the foundation of which is laid upon rocks rising some 20 feet out of the river. ROCK-ISLAND, N. of the junction of the Rock river with the Mississippi, is a flourishing village of 2,300 inhabitants. NAUVOO, the site of the Mormon city, which contained in its palmy days about 24,000 inhabitants, is located on a bluff, with an easy ascent. The Mormons have been driven out, and their magnificent temple was destroyed by fire in 1848. The city, or rather its ruins have been purchased by M. Cabet, the chief of the "Icarians," large bodies of which sect are now emigrating from France. WARSAW, opposite the mouth of the Des Moines river, is a small, but thriving village. QUINCY is situated on a bluff, and commands a fine view of the river and surrounding country. It has a large river trade, being the depôt of a fertile back-country. Pop. 7,000. ALTON, situated a little north of and opposite to the mouth of the Missouri, is a very thriving town, in a region rich in timber and bituminous coal. Population 4,500. KASKASKIA, on the river of the same name, 11 miles from its mouth, stands on an extensive plain. It was originally settled by the French from Canada, and was a place of the greatest importance. Population 1,800.

CAIRO, at the mouth of the Ohio, occupies a site most appropriate for a large commercial city, but in consequence of the lowness of the ground, and unhealthiness of the situation, it can never rise to that importance its projectors anticipated. A levee has been built to keep back the waters, at a cost of a million of dollars. Population from 200 to 300.

SHAWNEETOWN, on the Ohio, 9 miles S. of the Wabash, was originally a village occupied by Indians of the Shawnee tribe. It has considerable trade, and a population of 1,764

Among the interior towns the most notable are—OTTAWA, on Fox river, an important canal station; PERU, the western terminus of the Illinois and Michigan Canal; PEORIA, on the Illinois river, S. of Peoria Lake; PONTIAC, on Vermillion river; BLOOMINGTON, the county seat of McLean; BEARDSTOWN, on the Illinois; MEREDOSIA, on the same river; JACKSONVILLE, the seat of Illinois College; VANDALIA, on the National Road, &c. &c.

Early in the 17th century, Illinois was explored by La Salle, the enterprising traveller; and French settlements were formed at Kaskaskia, Cahokia, and other places soon afterwards. In 1763 the whole country was ceded to England. Until 1809, Illinois was a part of the territory N. W. of the Ohio. In that year it was placed under a separate territorial government, and in 1818 was admitted into the Union as a state. The present population has resulted from immigration during the current century.

THE STATE OF MISSOURI.

Area 67,380 *square miles.—Population* 682,044.

MISSOURI, the largest of the western states, is situated between 36° 30′ and 40° 30′ N. lat., and between 89° and 96° 45′ W. long.: and is bounded N. by Iowa; E. by Illinois and Kentucky, from which it is separated by the Mississippi river; S. by Arkansas, and W. by Nebraska Territory and the Missouri river.

Missouri has, generally, a rolling or hilly surface, and is about equally divided between prairie and timber land. The S. E. corner is almost entirely alluvial. No part of the state can be called mountainous. A range of low hills, however, commences in St. François county, and extends in a S. W. direction to the southern boundary; and another range, of a larger class, extends from the Missouri river, between the Gasconade and Osage, increasing in magnitude until far within the state of Arkansas. These are sometimes called the Ozark Mountains. The celebrated Iron mountain is situated in St. François county. Five miles S. of this is "Pilot Knob," also composed almost wholly of oxide of iron. These, with the exception of the recently discovered iron beds in northern Michigan, are the richest known deposits of iron in the world. Copper is found in several districts, and lead mines of great extent are known to exist. Washington county is a perfect bed of metallic wealth—lead, copper, copperas, black-lead, and brimstone; carnelian and other precious stones; free-stone, grind-stone, and burr-stone, and chalk, are the prevailing formations. St. Genevieve county has quarries of fine marble, and vast caverns full of beautiful white sand resembling snow, much prized for the manufacture of flint-glass. Throughout the mineral district beds of rich red marls are found, which prove to be the very best kind of manure, and such deposits being found in this comparatively sterile region are doubly valuable. The best portion of the state south of the Missouri river, is between the Osage and that river. It is agreeably diversified and fertile beyond conception, and abounds in coal, salt, &c. The country north of the Missouri is scarcely inferior. There is no part of the globe where greater extent of country can be traversed more easily when in its natural state. It has, for the most part, a surface delightfully rolling and variegated, sometimes rising into picturesque hills, and then stretching far away into the sea of prairie, occasionally interspersed with shady groves and sparkling streamlets.

The Mississippi meanders along the eastern border of the state for 400 miles, receiving in its course the turbid waters of the Missouri, which river traverses the state in a south-western direction. The La Mine, Osage, and Gasconade, from the S., and the Little Platte, Grand, and Chariton, from the N., are the navigable tributaries of the Missouri. Salt river, a navigable stream, falls into the Mississippi 86 miles above the mouth of the Missouri; and Maramee river, also navigable, disembogues 18 miles below St. Louis. The White Water and St. François drain the S. E. portion, and the tributaries of the Neosho the S. W. part of the state. The Missouri river, during a part of the year, is navigable for 1,800 miles.

Almost every acre of this fine country is susceptible of agricultural improvement. The climate is remarkably serene and temperate, being well suited to out-door employment and the raising of live-stock. The chief products consist of tobacco, hemp, wheat, oats, and Indian corn. Wool-growing is becoming a favorite employment; and of late years the improvement of breed has been attended to. The trade in hogs is very extensive, and large numbers of cattle are reared for the market. About five-sixths of the people are farmers. Mining occupies at least 4,000 persons, and perhaps two-thirds of these are employed at the lead mines: the remainder are employed at the iron, copper, and bituminous coal mines. As a manufacturing state Missouri is not of much importance. The exports from this state consist chiefly of agricultural produce and its minerals. Cattle and horses are also largely exported to the East and South. St. Louis is the chief commercial city, and the great receiving and distributing depôt. Internal trade is carried on mainly by steamboats on the Missouri and its tributaries.

The University of St. Louis, Kemper College, at the same place, and Missouri University, at Columbia, to each of which is attached a medical school, are the principal scholastic institutions. There are also colleges at Cape Girardeau, in Marion county, at St. Charles, and Fayette, and a medical college at Willoughby. Academies and common schools are supported on a liberal footing.

Missouri is divided into 106 counties. The principal cities and towns are Jefferson City, St. Louis, St. Charles, &c.

Jefferson City, the capital, is situated on the S. bank of the Missouri, 136 miles from its mouth, and near the center of the state. The State House and the Penitentiary are the principal public buildings. Population 4,000. The most important places on the river, W. of the capital, are Marion, Nashville, Rocheport, Booneville, Chariton, Lexington, Blayton, Liberty, Independence, Weston, St. Joseph's, &c. Independence, on the S. bank of the river, 352 miles from its junction with the Mississippi, is the starting-point or rendezvous for traders to northern Mexico, and for emigrants to Oregon and California. The distance from

4*

St. Louis by land is 266 miles. Portland, Pinkney, Newport, and St. Charles, lie eastward of Jefferson City. St. Charles, formerly the state capital, 22 miles from the mouth of the river on its N. bank, is a thriving place, and contains about 5,000 inhabitants, many of whom are of French origin. Warsaw and Osceola are the principal towns on Osage river.

St. Louis, the commercial capital of the state, and one of the most important places in the West, is situated on the Mississippi, 18 miles below the mouth of the Missouri, 863 miles from Fort Snelling, and 1,212 from New Orleans. No city could be better located for an extensive commerce. The whole Union is its tributary, and already its trade amounts to nearly one half the whole foreign commerce of the U. S. in value. About 1,000 flat-boats arrive here annually, and steamboats with an aggregate of 500,000 tons. The Illinois, Missouri, Ohio, and Mississippi are navigated by its fleets, and even the northern lakes contribute to its commerce. Year by year its importance is increasing. The city consists of two parts, built at different elevations. The lower part, or that on the margin of the river, is laid out in narrow streets, and is chiefly occupied by those engaged in business. The more elevated portion is different in appearance, and is laid out regularly in broad handsome streets, lined with the splendid mansions of the rich. A variety of public buildings beautify this locality. The population, about 77,860, is composed of men of all nations, but the most numerous are Americans, French, and Germans. The city is supplied with water from the river, which is raised into a reservoir by steam-power, and thence distributed through iron pipes. The streets are lighted with gas. St. Louis is the principal depôt of the American Fur Company. *Jefferson Barracks*, the most extensive military station in the West, is situated on a range of bluffs, about 9 miles below the city. The principal places N. of St. Louis are Westport, Clarkesville, Louisiana, Hannibal, Marion City, La Grange and Tully, on the Mississippi, and St. Francisville, on the Des Moines river. To the S. of St. Louis are Herculaneum and St. Genevieve, the chief ports of the mineral district; Cape Girardeau, which has a fine harbor for keel-boats; Ohio City, opposite Cairo, and New Madrid, formerly a noted place, but containing now less than 800 inhabitants.

Missouri was originally a portion of Louisiana, as purchased by the United States in 1803. Settlements were made at St. Louis, St. Genevieve, and elsewhere, about the middle of the last century. In 1821, Missouri became a state. Previous to its admission, however, great debate was had on the subject of slavery, nor was it until a distinctive line had been drawn between *slave soil* and *free soil* that the state was recognised by Congress. This line (36° 30′ N. lat.) is usually called the "Missouri Compromise line," N. of which to the Rocky Mountains, except so far as regards this state, slavery is never to be tolerated.

THE STATE OF IOWA.

Area 50,914 *square miles.—Population* 192,214.

IOWA is situated between 40° 30′ and 43° 30′ N. lat., and between 90° 20′ and 97° 40′ W. long.: and is bounded N. by Minesota Territory; E. by the Mississippi river, which separates it from Wisconsin and Illinois; S. by Missouri, and W. by the territory of Nebraska.

Prairie predominates in this state. Scarcely a hill interrupts the sea-like expanse of its wavy surface. An elevated table-land or plateau, however, extends through a considerable portion of the country, and forms the watershed between the streams flowing into the Missouri and Mississippi rivers respectively. The margins of the streams are thickly timbered. The prairie lands are variously covered: some are clothed in thick grass, suitable for grazing farms, while hazel thickets and sassafras shrubs invest others with perennial verdure. In spring and summer the surface is enamelled by wild flowers in endless variety. The soil is universally good, being a rich black mould, mixed sometimes with sandy loam, and sometimes with red clay and gravel. Lead, zinc, iron, &c., are very plentiful. The "mineral region" is principally confined to the neighborhood of Dubuque. The lead mines of this region are perhaps the most productive and valuable in the world. Ten thousand miners could here find profitable employment. Zinc occurs in fissures along with the lead, chiefly in the form of electric calamine. In some "diggings" this mineral is found in a state of carbonate, and in others as a sulphuret. Iron ore is abundant in several districts; but as yet the mines have not been worked to any great extent. The state is well watered by numerous navigable rivers and streamlets flowing into the Mississippi and Missouri rivers, which bound the state—the first on the E. and the latter on the W. The principal of these are the Red Cedar and Iowa, and the Des Moines, which empty into the Mississippi. The rivers falling into the Missouri are comparatively unimportant. The climate is excellent, especially on the prairies, and the country is as free from endemic diseases as the most favored portion of the Union. Periodic breezes blow over the prairies as regularly and as refreshing as on the ocean between the tropics. The only unhealthy portions of Iowa are the low margins of the rivers, which are frequently inundated. Though the buffalo, once the denizen of this beautiful country, is now almost extinct, and though the elk is only found in the wild recesses not yet occupied by civilization, a great variety of wild animals remain, and afford pleasure to the sportsman and profit to the hunter. The wolf, panther, and wild-cat are still numerous, and in the wooded districts the black bear is found. Foxes, racoons, opossums, gophars, porcupines, squirrels, and the otter, inhabit almost the whole unsettled country. Deer are also quite numerous, and the musk-rat and common rabbit are incredibly prolific. Among the bird tribes are wild-turkeys, prairie-hens, grouse, partridges, woodcocks, &c. Geese, ducks, loons, pelicans, plovers, snipes, &c., are among the aquatic birds that visit the rivers, lakes, and sluices. Bees swarm in the forests; the rivers and creeks abound with excellent fish, and the insect tribes, varied and beautiful, add gaudiness to the scene.

Iowa mainly owes its prosperity to its agricultural resources. Its fine prairies are easily converted to cultivation, and its natural pastures afford peculiar facilities for the rearing of cattle, and sheep farming. Wool-growing, indeed, has become one of the staple employments of the farmers; and the raising of hogs for market, is no less profitable in its results. The sheep and hog are here raised with little or no trouble, the natural productions of the forest and prairie affording a plentiful subsistence. The cereal and root crops grow luxuriantly, and all the fruits of temperate climates find here a congenial soil. Tobacco is grown extensively on the alluvial margins of the Des Moines, and the castor-oil plant, which has been lately introduced, succeeds well. No country in the world, in every point of view, is more promising to the agriculturist. Fertile and productive, yielding minerals of the greatest value, penetrated by numerous navigable rivers, and bordered by the noble Mississippi, easily accessible, and free from many of the dangers incident to newly-settled countries, it offers the greatest inducements to immigrants and others to make it their homes. Its commercial advantages are perhaps second to those of none other of the Western States, while every portion of the country is open to easy navigation and land travel. It already contributes largely to the valuable cargoes that annually arrive at New Orleans. The settled portion of the state is well provided with good roads; but as yet no canals or railroads, though several are projected, have been built. The manufactures of Iowa consist principally of such heavy articles as are of immediate necessity to the settler, or of such goods as are usually made in families, as coarse woollen and cotton articles, &c. The aggregate value of property assessed for taxes in this state in 1852 was $38,427,376.

Education is well provided for. A respectable university has been established, and the constitution makes it imperative that a school shall be established in each district. Instruction is placed under the direction of a superintendent, chosen by the people for three years. The permanent school fund amounted, Nov. 1st, 1852, to $500,000, and all lands granted by Congress, all escheated estates, and all rents accruing from unsold lands of the state, are applied to this fund, the interest of which is devoted exclusively to the support of schools. Military exemption fines, and all fines imposed by courts, are appropriated to the same purpose. The University is supported by the interest of moneys arising from the lease or sale of public lands granted by Congress for the support of the institution.

The settled portion of Iowa is divided into 102 counties. Among the principal cities and towns are Iowa City, Dubuque, Muscatine, Burlington, Keokuck, &c.

IOWA CITY, the capital, is situated on the E. bank of the Iowa river, about 60 miles N. of its junction with Red Cedar river. The river is navigable to this point for keel-boats. The location is beautiful, rising in a succession of plateaux or elevated terraces, overlooking a splendid country. Previous to 1839 the site was in the wilderness. The state capitol is a handsome building in the Doric style of architecture. It is 120 feet long and 60 feet wide, and is two stories high above the basement, and surmounted by a dome supported by 16 Corinthian columns. The churches and many of the private residences are substantially built, and in some cases elegantly. Population in 1850, 1,582.

DUBUQUE, on the Mississippi river, 1712 miles from its mouth, and 468 from the Falls of St. Anthony, is situated in the very center of the lead region, and is the chief outlet for the commerce of the district. It was originally settled by a French half-breed of the name of Dubuque. It is regularly laid out, and has a city charter. It contains six or seven churches, one of which is an elegant Roman Catholic cathedral of stone. Considerable commerce is attracted to this place, and the trade of the city has long been in a flourishing condition. The Land Office for the District, and the Surveyor-General's Office for the states of Iowa and Wisconsin, are located here. The interior of the state contributes largely of its agricultural wealth to swell its otherwise commercial prosperity. Population 4,071. DAVENPORT, 74 miles S. of Dubuque, is finely located on an elevated plain, and surrounded by a rich agricultural country. It is becoming an important place of trade. Pop. 3,400. MUSCATINE, formerly Bloomington, 22 miles further south, is one of the most thriving towns in the state, and contains a court house, jail, several churches, and a number of mercantile houses and stores. Population 2,534. In 1840, the population was less than 600. BURLINGTON, 248 miles above St. Louis, formerly the territorial capital, is finely situated for an extended trade. It was originally laid out in 1833. The ground rises gradually from the river to the hills which form its background. It contains many fine public buildings. A steam-ferry here crosses the Mississippi. The site was formerly known as the Flint Hills, an old Indian trading-post, and was once the residence of Black Hawk, whose remains are buried here. Population 5,129. FORT MADISON, 10 miles below Burlington, has a population of about 2,000. KEOKUCK, a few miles N. of the mouth of the Missouri, is becoming rapidly an important place, and has, of late years, increased in population and wealth, perhaps more than any other town in the state. It has a large commerce, and many advantages in situation and topography, which must ultimately make it a most flourishing mart. The present population is 2,773.

The interior towns are in general small, consisting chiefly of agricultural settlements. SALEM, in Henry county, is a thriving settlement, and chiefly inhabited by members of the Society of Friends. A considerable colony of Mormons is settled in Pottawatamie county.

Iowa was a portion of Louisiana as purchased in 1803. It was erected into a separate territorial government in 1838, and admitted into the Union as a state in 1846.

THE STATE OF WISCONSIN.

Area 53,924 *square miles.—Population* 305,891.

WISCONSIN lies between 42° 30′ and 47° N. lat., and between 87° and 92° 30′ W. long.: and is bounded N. by Lake Superior and the northern peninsula of Michigan; E. by Lake Michigan; S. by Illinois, and W. by Iowa and Minesota Territory.

Wisconsin is one vast plain, varied only by river hills and the gentle swells and undulations of the country. This plain is elevated from 600 to 1,500 feet above the level of the ocean. The highest lands are the watershed between the waters flowing respectively to the Mississippi and Lake Michigan. The slope towards Lake Superior is very abrupt, and the rivers short, rapid, and broken by falls. The Wisconsin and Mississippi bluffs rise from 100 to 300 feet above the rivers. The soil is excellent, black marl predominating in the lowest timber and prairie lands, and is often six feet deep. The dark loam is the most common in the openings and on the rolling prairie, and is cultivated with the best success. The country is naturally divided into timbered, opening, and prairie. South-east of the Fox and Wisconsin it is in general heavily wooded. In the mineral region S. of the Wisconsin, the rolling prairie, interspersed with openings, prevails. North of these rivers the country is pretty equally divided between openings and prairie. The climate is mild and salubrious, and perhaps more congenial to the European constitution than that of any other of the United States.

Geologically, Wisconsin presents interesting phenomena. The northern portion is entirely primitive, and exhibits granite and old red sandstone as its bases. The Wisconsin flows through the sandstone district, and the hills on this river are soft and crumbling, and when carried into the stream by a rise of water, frequently change its current. The mineral district occupies the S. W. corner of the state. Wisconsin has great advantages in the availability and easy transport of its mineral wealth. The production of galena has become very considerable, and the copper mines of the north and west are prospectively of immense value. Many other metals are found, and good marble and building stone are abundant in almost every part.

Besides the great lakes on the N. and W., a number of smaller lakes, varying from one to twenty miles in extent, are scattered over the state. These are often surrounded by the most beautiful scenery, and abound in fish of various kinds, while on their shores are found fine specimens of agate, carnelian, and other precious stones. In the shoal waters of the bays the *zigania aquatica*, a species of wild rice, is abundant, and attracts immense flocks of water-fowl to these localities. Green Bay, in the N. E., is a large arm of Lake Michigan, and receives the Fox and other rivers. The Mississippi forms a large part of the W. boundary. It is augmented from this state by the Chippewa and Wisconsin rivers, the latter of which, with the Fox river, divides the state into two nearly equal portions. Innumerable smaller streams and branches run through the whole extent of the state, so that no portion of it is without a plentiful supply of good, and generally, pure water. The Wisconsin and Chippewa are navigable for steamboats.

All kinds of crops that are raised in temperate climates may be cultivated with success in Wisconsin; and owing to the great range of pasturage on the prairies, it is an uncommonly fine grazing country. Already it exports largely of grain. Manufactures are still in their infancy. But few countries have the same natural facilities for extensive operations, and there can be no doubt, that as the wants of the people enlarge, these will be made subservient to their interests. The ports on Lake Michigan are already distinguished for their busy commerce, and their rapid increase in prosperity and wealth. The river trade is great, and the busy strife of commercial activity has penetrated to the very centre of the state. Steamboats ply on its waters, and a system of good roads greatly facilitates the development of its natural capacities. The union of the waters of Lake Michigan with those of the Mississippi, by canaling the portage between the Fox and Wisconsin rivers, is now almost realized, and will, when completed, create a navigable channel of the greatest importance. Wisconsin has also several railroads, which together will extend over a line of 800 miles, about 60 of which are now in operation.

Wisconsin has made provision for an extensive system of education. The Wisconsin University, at Madison, was established in 1849. The number of school districts is 3,200, and the number of children in the state between 4 and 20 years of age about 124,000. The school fund consists of the proceeds of the 16th sections of land, 500,000 acres ceded to the state by Congress; all forfeitures and escheats to the state; all military exemption fines; all the net proceeds of penal fines; 5 per cent. of the proceeds of all sales of U. S. lands in the state, and all moneys arising from any grant to the state, where the purposes of such grant are not specified. The value of these various items is not ascertained, but must be great and ever increasing.

The state is divided into 46 counties, 18 of which are S. of the Fox and Wisconsin rivers. N. of these the settlements are very sparse. The most important cities and towns are Madison, Milwaukee, Sheboygan, Manitouwoc, Green Bay, Mineral Point, &c.

Madison, the capital, 90 miles W. of Milwaukee, is pleasantly situated between the 3d and 4th of the chain called "Four Lakes," on a gently rising ground, from which there is a regular descent each way to the water. It is regularly laid out, with a central square, in the middle of which stands the State House. This is a spacious stone edifice, two stories high above the basement, and surmounted with a handsome dome, and can be seen for a distance of 10 miles from every direction. The city also contains the county prison and several churches, with a number of stores. Two newspapers are issued weekly. Population 2,000. It was laid out in 1836.

Milwaukee, the largest and most important town of the state, is situated on both sides of Milwaukee river, near its entrance into Lake Michigan, 90 miles N. of Chicago, Ill. It is the natural outlet of one of the finest grain regions in the Union. The progress of the city has been most remarkable. In 1834 it was surrounded by a wilderness, and contained only two log-houses. It has now 26,000 inhabitants, and for the last few years has increased at the rate of 2,000 or 3,000 annually. Regular lines of steamboats ply between Milwaukee and Buffalo, the trade between which is immense, and constantly increasing. Sheboygan, at the entrance of Sheboygan river into Lake Michigan, 56 miles N. of Milwaukee, has a deep and capacious harbor, and is a place of rising importance. Manitouwoc, 30 miles further N., is also a rapidly progressing village. Population 766. In 1849 it imported goods to the amount of $127,000, and exported agricultural produce to the value of $72,000. Racine and Washington are also towns well situated, and have a prospect of attaining commercial prosperity. Green Bay, at the head of the bay of the same name, and on the E. bank of the Fox river, at its mouth, is a most important haven; and when the improvements in the Fox and Wisconsin rivers are completed, so as to admit of navigation through the state to the Mississippi, it must rapidly increase in population and wealth. Fort Howard, on the opposite bank of the river, is one of the most important military stations in the north-west.

Prairie du Chien, on the Mississippi, is the most prominent point on that river. It is situated a few miles N. of the Wisconsin river, and has its name from the beautiful prairie on which it is located. It is one of the oldest settlements in the west, and has been the scene of many battles, both of Indian and civilized warfare. The Indian trade that once centered here, has almost ceased since the removal of the Winnebagoes. Population about 2,000. MINERAL POINT, 50 miles W. of Madison; FOND DU LAC, at the head of Winnebago Lake; ELKHORN, 22 miles W. of Racine; and MONROE, 30 miles S. E. of Mineral Point, are important interior towns. FORT WINNEBAGO is situated at the portage between the Fox and Wisconsin rivers, and on the great route between the lakes and the Mississippi. This portage will be overcome by a canal now in process of completion. There are also, in the interior counties, a large number of villages, with populations varying from 300 to 700; and so rapidly are new villages being settled, that it is next to an impossibility to take account of them. In many instances large colonies of Germans, Norwegians, and other European emigrants, have purchased tracts of land, and built up their villages as if by magic; and the immediate neighbors are even ignorant of their presence, until they behold with astonishment the smoke curling over the new settlement.

Wisconsin originally belonged to the French, and formed part of that vast territory known as "New France," which was ceded to Great Britain in 1763. Few settlements were made previous to 1836, when it was erected into a separate territorial government. In 1848 it was admitted as a state into the Union. Never since the formation of the American Confederacy has a state advanced so rapidly in population: the tide of immigration is continuous not only from Europe but from the eastern United States, and certainly few states have ever before presented such a combination of inducements to those seeking a home. Its situation and facilities of intercourse, its agricultural capacities, its mineral wealth, and other natural advantages are pre-eminently inviting, and offer golden prospects to every grade and condition of man.

THE TERRITORY OF MINESOTA.

Area 141,839 *square miles.—Population* 6,077.

MINESOTA is situated between 43° 30′ and 49° N. lat., and between 89° 30′ and 102° 10′ W. long.: and is bounded N. by British America; E. by Lake Superior and the state of Wisconsin; S. by the state of Iowa, and W. by Missouri Territory. Of the immense territory included within these limits, 22,336 square miles belonged to the late territory of Wisconsin, and the remainder to the late territory of Iowa.

Throughout the whole of this territory scarcely an elevation that could be dignified with the name of mountain occurs. The surface is in general level or undulating, but varies considerably in elevation, and in the ascents and descents of its plateaux. In some parts, especially in the neighborhood of the Mississippi and St. Peter's, the ground is much broken, and their margins lined with high bluffs of various formations; while in others the rivers flow through deep channels, seemingly worn into the earth by the force of their waters. Every portion of Minesota may be reached by inland navigation. The traveller will meet constantly with springs and small lakes, the sources of mighty rivers, whose waters are discharged thousands of miles to the N. into Hudson's Bay; as many to the E. into the Gulf of St. Lawrence, or to the S. into the Gulf of Mexico. Springs are often seen within a few feet of each other, the sources of rivers, whose outlets in the ocean are some six thousand miles apart. In almost every direction canoe navigation, with short portages, is practicable by means of the numerous rivers, whose sources are nearly interlocked or connected by chains of lakes. The Mississippi has its source here, some 3,000 miles from its mouth. Nine hundred miles of the length of this majestic river are embraced in this territory, and its numerous tributaries course through its fertile plains. The N. E. portion is washed by the crystal waters of Lake Superior, which is of itself an inland sea for the prosecution of trade and commerce, and opens an avenue to the Atlantic. The Missouri, after having flowed nearly 1,000 miles from the base of the Rocky Mountains, sweeps along its whole W. boundary, ensuring navigation almost to Oregon. Its large tributaries, James and Big Sioux rivers, water valleys of great beauty and fertility. Extensive prairies, blooming with flowers and covered with luxuriant grasses, affording sustenance to immense herds of buffalo, saying nothing of elk, deer, antelopes, and other small game. Red River, which discharges itself into Lake Winnipeg, has its sources near those of the Mississippi. Beautiful lakes of transparent water, well stocked with fish, and varying in size from ponds to inland seas, are profusely scattered over the territory. Forests of pine and other evergreens, orchards of sugar-maple, groves of hard and soft woods of various species, wild rice and cranberries, and various species of wild fruit, copious springs of pure water, a fertile soil, and water-power, easily improved and abundantly distributed, render this region peculiarly adapted to the wants of man. Add to these a salubrious climate, and Minesota appears to enjoy eminent capacities for becoming a thriving and populous state. Its mineral resources are unknown, but indications and discoveries have been made that certify its wealth in copper and lead. Building stone of every description, limestone, &c., are found everywhere underlying the soil, while many valuable and precious stones are found on the shores of the lakes. For a country so overspread with lakes, and traversed by such a number of rivers, it is astonishingly free from marsh and morass. The land has a great elevation above the Gulf of Mexico, and the waters of the N. and E., and as a consequence is easily and perfectly drained; and moreover, the margins of the lakes and rivers themselves are generally surrounded by hills and bluffs, which protect their neighborhoods from inundation. The whole country is thus eligible for agriculture.

The settlements as yet made in the territory are chiefly confined to the peninsula between the Mississippi and St. Croix on the S., and on the Red river on the N. Otherwise the country is inhabited only by the aboriginal hunters, the Chippewas, and Sioux Indians. Their numbers are not ascertained, but may approximate to about 12,000. With some of the tribes treaties have been made for the purchase of their lands, and for their removal, which, when effected, will open to the white settler immense tracts of rich and fertile soils, productive of every species of grain and fruits usually grown in northern climates. The Indians have long been in connection with the whites, and have for more than two centuries carried on with them a profitable trade in furs and peltries. Their hunting-grounds are now chiefly confined to the vast prairies west of the Mississippi. The white inhabitants are from almost every portion of the world: the Canadian, the sons of New England and the Middle States, with English, French, and Germans, are all intermingled; and not a few of the citizens consist of half-breeds, who chiefly reside on the Red River, and have settlements for some distance on both sides of our N. boundary. These are descendants of the original settlers at Lord Selkirk's colony and Indian women of the Chippewa family Their village is called Pembina. Hardy and hard working, prudent as the New England farmer, religious and intelligent, they form no mean class in the general community. They trade with the southern settlers, exchanging furs and pemmican for the superfluities of the South. They rear cattle and sheep, weave their own clothing, and live in a middle state of civilization. They have churches and schools, and many of the better class are educated at a collegiate establishment which has long been maintained among them. As a consequence, however, of their ostracized situation, they still retain many of the peculiarities of their original nations, modified indeed by the circumstances that surround them, and their connection with savage life. In the new settlements, the industry of the whites is almost entirely agricultural. They have mills on a number of the streams, and steamboats ply regularly on their waters. They are building roads, and from the energy they exhibit in overcoming natural obstacles, the real prosperity of the territory seems to be ensured. A large business has been already done by the steamboats that sail regularly between Galena and St. Paul and Stillwater. The products of the chase, and the fruits of the field are exported in considerable quantities. With regard to immigration, the prospects are favorable. Farmers, laborers, and professional men, are daily ascending the rivers in search of a new home. The day indeed is not distant, when the forests will be laid low, and the flowery prairies be converted into fields and gardens, producing every necessary to the use and enjoyment of man. Earth, air, and water abound in the prerequisites of man's happiness and enjoyment, and are only awaiting his advent to yield up their now unused abundance.

The organization of the government of the territory having been so recent, it is impossible to exhibit by statistics the resources of this new and almost untouched country. The first legislature, which adjourned after a session of sixty days, on the 1st November, 1849, was chiefly employed in organizing the government, and dividing the territory into suitable civil districts, and appointing officers to enforce the laws. Among its most important acts were those establishing the judiciary, a school system, and relative to the improvement of roads. All these will have a paramount influence over the future destiny of the country. Perhaps one of the most humane and politic acts of the legislature was the admission to citizenship of "all persons of a mixture of white and Indian blood, who shall have adopted the habits and customs of civilized men;" and not less politic is that law which requires the establishment of schools throughout the territory. The act of the General Government organizing the territory appropriates two sections of land in every township for the support of common schools. No other state in the Union has received more than one section in each township for such purpose. On the 11th June, 1849, the whole citizen population numbered 4,780, of which 3,067 were males and 1,713 females. In 1850 it amounted to 6,077, and at the present time (March, 1854) can not be less than 12,000.

Minesota was divided by the Legislature into 20 counties in lieu of the counties of St. Croix and La Pointe, which constituted the remaining portions of the territories of Iowa and Wisconsin, of which Minesota was formed. The principal settlements are St. Paul, Stillwater, Mendota, Fort Snelling, Pembina, &c.

St. Paul, the capital, is situated on the left bank of the Mississippi, 15 miles by water, and 8 miles by land, below the Falls of St. Anthony. The town is situated on a plateau terminating on the river in a precipitous bluff 80 feet elevation above the river. The bluff recedes from the river at the upper and lower ends of the town, forming two landings, from both of which the ascent is gradual. The first store or trading-house was built in 1842. In June, 1849, the town contained 142 houses, all of which, with the exception of perhaps a dozen, had been built within the year previous. This number included the Government House, three hotels, four warehouses, ten stores, several groceries, two printing-offices, (from which two newspapers are issued weekly,) several mechanics' shops, a school-house, &c. There was not a brick or stone house in the town. Since the period above mentioned, however, several churches and many durable houses, built of stone and brick, from materials in the vicinity, have been erected. The population in June, 1850, was 1,112 St. Paul is well located for commerce; and from its being at the head of navigation below the Falls, must necessarily become not only the political, but the commercial capital of the territory. In the neighborhood of St. Paul there is an extensive settlement of Canadians, chiefly persons formerly employed by the Hudson Bay Company, called LITTLE CANADA. Population 600.

STILLWATER is situated on the W. side of Lake St. Croix, near its head, on ground having a gentle ascent from the shore to a high bluff in the rear, which extends in the form of a crescent, and nearly encloses the town. The first settlement was made in 1843. It contains a Court House, several hotels and stores, and many neat dwellings. Steamboats seldom ascend higher than this place. The environs consist of a beautiful prairie country, and are being rapidly brought under cultivation. Population in June, 1849, 609. MARINE MILLS is a flourishing settlement on St. Croix river, a few miles above its entrance into the lake. The precinct contains about 200 inhabitants. Its water-power and the fine country which surrounds it must enforce its speedy increase and prosperity. Several villages on the Wisconsin side of the St. Croix river have been established, and are rapidly increasing in importance. Indeed, the resources of the vicinity on both sides are such as to ensure to the villages considerable commerce.

FORT SNELLING is situated on the high rocky promontory, 106 feet above the water, at the confluence of St. Peter's river with the Mississippi. The military works were commenced in 1819. The fort is in the form of a hexagon and surrounded by a stone wall. From the river its appearance is imposing and seemingly impregnable. It is, however, within the reach of cannon from higher ground: but the object for which the site was selected—the protection of the frontier from savage incursion—is well attained by its situation. The garrison usually consists of three companies of dragoons. The view from these fortifications is extensive. The military reservation of the establishment embraces an area of 10 miles square, of which the fort is near the center. The settlement in the neighborhood contains only about 40 inhabitants. In the fort there were 267 males and 50 females in June, 1849. MENDOTA, or St. Peter's, on the W. bank of the Mississippi, S. of the confluence of St. Peter's river, has been occupied for several years by the American Fur Company as a depôt for their trading establishments with the Indians of the north-west. Two stores and two or three houses constitute the village. It is, however, a fine town site; and being situated at the junction of two great rivers, and near the head of steam navigation, its importance in a commercial point of view has not been overlooked. Whites are not allowed to reside here without special permission from the U. S. government, the village being in the military reservation. It will ultimately command the trade of the St. Peter's river. Population in June, 1849, 122.

Some other small villages exist in this neighborhood, but of their importance or present state little is known. KAPOSIA, from its situation near the point of land opposite St. Paul, though yet little more than an Indian town, may ultimately become of consequence. ST. ANTHONY, at the Falls, and SAUK RAPIDS, opposite the mouth of Osakis river, are both on the E. bank of the Mississippi; and higher up, on both sides of Nokay river, is FORT GAINES, the most northerly military establishment in the country. The supplying of these remote stations with provisions, &c., creates considerable traffic and travelling both by land and water. The return traffic consists of furs and peltry, with other Indian contributions.

The territory of Minesota derives its name from *Mini-sotah*, the Indian name for St. Peter's river; *mini* in their language meaning "water," and *sotah* "muddy or slightly turbid." The country originally belonged to the French by priority of discovery. At an early period their traders, missionaries, and soldiers had penetrated into the western wilderness. The United States had little authority over this region until 1812. In 1816 a law of Congress excluded foreigners from the Indian trade; and for the encouragement of our citizens the military post at Fort Snelling was established in 1819. Among the explorers of this country the names of Carver, Pike, Cass, Long, Beltrami, Schoolcraft, Nicollet, Owen, &c., will ever be intimately connected with its history. The honor of verifying the sources of the Mississippi belongs to Schoolcraft. The present territory was established by act of Congress, 3d March, 1849, and shortly after Alexander Ramsey was appointed Governor, and made St. Paul his capital, where the government was organized. "Congress may hereafter divide said territory, or annex any portion of it to another state or territory."

THE WESTERN TERRITORY

This territory comprises the remaining unorganized portion of Louisiana, as purchased by the United States in 1803. It extends from the Nebraska or Platte river northward to the 49th parallel, and from White Earth and Missouri rivers westward to the Rocky Mountains. The territory has an area of 724,264 square miles.

The greater part of this immense territory is watered by the Missouri river and its numerous tributaries. The Yellow Stone, the largest tributary, extends its branches to the very base of the Rocky Mountains, and to near the sources of the Nebraska. A mountain ridge, which branches from the great Rocky Mountains, in about 42° N. lat., traverses the country in a N. E. direction towards Lake Winnipeg. In the E. portion of the territory the country is partly covered with forests, but beyond this commences a vast ocean of prairie, almost level, and clothed in grass and flowers. Approaching the mountains, however, the country gradually assumes a barren aspect. Countless droves of buffalo, elk, and deer, range upon the vast plains, but even these are fast diminishing before the attacks of the hunter.

In a country of such extent, generally level, naked, and open, the climate must in a great measure correspond to the latitude. Immediately on the borders of the settled states it is mild and temperate ; beyond, it gradually becomes more extreme, and towards the mountains cold, bleak, and polar. Travellers speak of encountering storms of hail and sleet in the summer. When the winds blow from the W. over the mountain summits, the cold they occasion is intense.

As yet the whole territory is inhabited by Indians, but the time is not far distant when the pioneer will penetrate its forests and prairies, and bring under cultivation the soil that from its creation has not been turned by the labor of man. The wild herds will be replaced by the ox, the horse, and the sheep, and golden crops will succeed the flowers and grasses that now only bloom in useless luxuriance, and wither with the first frosts of autumn, without contributing to the necessity or comfort of civilized man.

ROUTES IN THE

WESTERN STATES.

OHIO.

(1) CINCINNATI to PITTSBURG.

Steamboat.

Place	Miles	Total
Columbia, O.	5	
Little Miami River, O.	2	7
New Richmond, O.	12	19
Point Pleasant, O.	5	24
Moscow, O.	4	28
Mechanicsburg, Ky.	7	35
AUGUSTA, Ky.	7	42
Higginsport, O.	4	46
Ripley, O.	6	52
Charleston, Ky.	2	54
MAYSVILLE, Ky. Aberdeen, O.	8	62
Manchester, O.	12	74
Concord, Ky.	7	81
Rome, O.	5	86
Vanceburg, Ky.	7	93
Rockville, O.	4	97
PORTSMOUTH, O., (mouth of Scioto River)	16	113
Greenupsburg, Ky.	22	135
Hanging Rock, O.	6	141
Catlettsburg, Va.	14	155
Burlington, O.	4	159
Proctorsville, O. Guyandotte, Va.	8	167
Millersport, O.	13	180
Gallipolis, O.	24	204
Point Pleasant, Va., (mouth of Great Kanawha River)	4	208
Coalport, O. Sheffield, O.	12	220
Pomeroy, O.	1	221
Letartsville, O.	15	236
Ravenswood, Va.	22	258
Hockingsport, O.	21	279
Blennerhassett's Island	11	290
Belpre, O. Parkersburg, Va.	2	292
MARIETTA, O., (mouth of Muskingum River)	13	305
Newport, O.	17	322
Sisterville, Va.	25	347
Elizabethtown, Va.	37	384
WHEELING, VA. Bridgeport, O.	13	397
Warrenton, O.	9	406
Wellsburg, Va.	8	414
Steubenville, O.	7	421
Wellsville, O.	20	441
Liverpool, O.	4	445
Georgetown, Pa.	4	449
Beaver, Pa.	14	463
Freedom, Pa.	5	468
Economy, Pa.	6	474
Middletown, Pa.	12	486
PITTSBURG, PA.	11	497

(2) CINCINNATI to ST. LOUIS.

Place	Miles	Total
To North Bend, O.	16	
Great Miami River, O.	4	20
Lawrenceburg, Ia.	2	22
Aurora, Ia.	5	27
Belleview, Ky.	6	33
Rising Sun, Ia.	3	36
Hamilton, Ky.	11	47
Patriot, Ia.	2	49
Warsaw, Ky.	10	59
Vevay, Ia.	10	69
Mouth of Kentucky Riv., Ky.	10	79
MADISON, IA.	12	91
New London, Ia.	9	100
Westport, Ky.	15	115
Utica, Ia.	16	131
Jeffersonville, Ky.	8	139
LOUISVILLE, KY.	1	140
Shippingsport, Ky.	2	142
New Albany, Ia. Portland, Ky.	1	143
West Point, Ky.	20	163
Brandenburg, Ky.	17	180
Mauckport, Ia.	1	181
Northampton, Ia.	7	188
Amsterdam, Ia.	3	191
Leavensworth, Ia.	8	199
Fredonia, Ia.	4	203
Alton, Ia.	13	216
Concordia, Ky.	10	226

Stevensport, Ky. / Rome, Ia.	11	237
Cloversport, Ky.	10	247
Carmelton, Ia.	13	260
Troy, Ia.	6	266
Lewisport, Ky.	6	272
Rockport, Ia.	12	284
Owensburg, Ky.	9	293
Enterprise, Ia.	6	299
Newburg, Ia.	15	314
Green River, Ky.	6	320
EVANSVILLE, Ia.	8	328
Hendersonville, Ky.	10	338
Mount Vernon, Ia.	26	364
Uniontown, Ky.	15	379
Wabash River	5	384
Raleigh, Ky.	6	390
Shawneetown, Ill.	5	395
Caseyville, Ky.	9	404
Cave in Rock, Ill.	13	417
Elizabethtown, Ill.	7	424
Golconda, Ill.	12	436
Smithland, Ky., (mouth of Cumberland River)	18	454
Paducah, Ky., (mouth of Tennessee River)	15	469
Belgrade, Ill.	6	475
Fort Massac, Ill.	3	478
Caledonia, Ill.	24	502
Trinity, Ill.	9	511
CAIRO, ILL., (mouth of Ohio River)	5	516
Commerce, Mo.	28	544
Cape Girardeau, Mo.	12	556
Bainbridge, Mo.	12	568
Chester, Ill.	45	613
St. Genevieve, Mo.	16	629
Selma, Mo.	25	654
Herculaneum, Mo.	4	658
Harrisonville, Ill.	2	660
Jefferson Barracks, Mo.	19	679
ST. LOUIS, Mo.	9	688

(3) CINCINNATI to N. ORLEANS.

To Cairo, (mouth of Ohio River,) [see 2]	516	
NEW ORLEANS	1040	1556

(4) CINCINNATI to INDIANAPOLIS.

To Cheviot	7	
Miami	6	13
Clark's Store	4	17
Harrison	4	21
New Trenton, Ia.	6	27
Cedar Grove	5	32
Brookville	8	40
Metamora	7	47
Laurel	5	52
Andersonville	6	58
New Salem	4	62
Rushville	7	69
Beech Grove	7	76
Morristown	7	83
Kinder	6	89
Sugar Creek	5	94
INDIANAPOLIS	15	109

(5) CINCINNATI to ST. LOUIS.

Stage.

To Indianapolis, (see 8)	109	
ST. LOUIS, (see 86)	239	348

(6) CINCINNATI to PITTSBURG.

Stage via Steubenville.

To Columbus, (see 14)	127	
Zanesville, (see 15)	56	183
Cambridge, (see 15)	24	207
Winchester	9	216
Antrim	5	221
Londonderry	3	224
Smyrna	4	228
Moorefield	4	232
Cadiz	13	245
Greene	8	253
Bloomingdale	3	256
Wintersville	10	266
STEUBENVILLE	5	271
Holliday's Cove	3	274
Paris	4	278
Florence	5	283
Bavington	4	287
North Star	3	290
Fayette	6	296
PITTSBURG	13	309

(7) CINCINNATI to WHEELING, VA.

Stage.

To Columbus, (see 14)	127	
WHEELING, VA., (see 15)	130	257

(8) CINCINNATI to SANDUSKY CITY.

Little Miami R. R.

To Columbia	5	
Plainville	4	9
Milford	5	14
Germany	2	16
Polktown	2	18
Loveland's	2	20

Foster's	6	26
Deerfield	4	30
Morrow	5	35
Fort Ancient	4	39
Freeport	3	42
Waynesville	5	47
Claysville	4	51
Spring Valley	7	58
Xenia	7	65
Yellow Springs	10	75
SPRINGFIELD	10	85
Mad River and Lake Erie R. R.		
Urbana	14	99
West Liberty	10	109
Bellefontaine	8	117
Huntsville	7	124
Richland	3	127
Bell Centre	2	129
Kenton	12	141
Paterson	11	152
Cary	13	165
Oregon	5	170
Tiffin	11	181
Republic	9	190
Lodi	5	195
Bellevue	9	204
SANDUSKY CITY	15	219

(9) CINCINNATI to DAYTON.

Via Lebanon.

To Reading	10	
Sharonville	3	13
Pisgah	5	18
Mason	6	24
Lebanon	8	32
Ridgeville	7	39
Centreville	6	45
DAYTON	9	54

(10) CINCINNATI to DAYTON.

Via Franklin.

To Reading	10	
Sharonville	3	13
West Chester	5	18
Bethany	4	22
Monroe	4	26
Franklin	10	36
Miamisburg	6	42
Alexandersville	4	46
DAYTON	8	54

(11) CINCINNATI to CHILLICOTHE.

To Fulton	4	
Plainville	4	8
Milford	5	13
Perrin's Mills	5	18
Marathon	9	27
Fayetteville	8	35
Allensburg	8	43
Hillsboro'	10	53
Rainsboro'	10	63
Bainbridge	8	71
Bourneville	11	82
CHILLICOTHE	13	95

(12) CINCINNATI to ZANESVILLE.

To Walnut Hills	3	
Pleasant Ridge	5	8
Montgomery	5	13
Twenty Mile Stand	7	20
Hopkinsville	4	24
Morrow	3	27
Rochester	4	31
Clarksville	7	38
Wilmington	10	48
Sabino	10	58
Washington Court House	12	70
New Holland	10	80
Williamsport	8	88
Circleville	9	97
Amanda	12	109
LANCASTER	9	118
Rushville	9	127
Somerset	8	135
Fultonham	10	145
Putnam	10	155
ZANESVILLE	1	156

(13) CINCINNATI to EATON.

To Carthage	6	
Springdale	7	13
Hamilton	10	23
Rossville	1	24
Collinsville	8	32
Somerville	4	36
Camden	5	41
EATON	8	49

(14) CINCINNATI to SIDNEY.

To Carthage	6	
Springdale	7	13
Hamilton	10	23
Trenton	10	33
Middletown	4	37
Franklin	6	43
Miamisburg	6	49
Alexandersville	4	53
DAYTON	8	61
West Charleston	10	71
Troy	11	82
Piqua	7	89
SIDNEY	13	102

(15) CINCINNATI to COLUMBUS.

To Xenia, (see 8)	65	
Columbus and Xenia R. R.		
Cedarville	8	73
South Charleston	11	84
London	11	95
West Jefferson	10	105
COLUMBUS	14	119

(16) COLUMBUS to WHEELING, VA.

Central Ohio R. R.		
Black Lick	11	
Pataskala	6	17
Summit	5	22
Union	4	26
NEWARK	7	33
Clay Lick	6	39
Rockdale	2	41
Black Hand	5	46
Claypool Mill	4	50
Pleasant Valley	2	52
Dillons Falls	4	56
ZANESVILLE	3	59

(17) COLUMBUS to INDIANAPOLIS, IA.

To Alton	9	
West Jefferson	5	14
La Fayette	8	22
Summerford	5	27
Vienna	5	32
Springfield	10	42
Enon	7	49
Fairfield	7	56
DAYTON	11	67
Liberty	7	74
Medill	7	81
West Alexandria	6	87
Eaton	6	93
New Westerville	10	103
Richmond, Ia.	6	109
Centreville	6	115
Cambridge	9	124
Dublin	2	126
Lewisville	8	134
Knightstown	10	144
Charlotteville	5	149
Kinnard	4	153
Greenfield	4	157
Philadelphia	5	162
Cumberland	5	167
INDIANAPOLIS	10	177

(18) COLUMBUS to LOWER SANDUSKY.

To Clintonville	4	
Worthington	5	9
Williamsville	6	15
Delaware	9	24
Norton	10	34
Waldo	6	40
Marion	3	43
Little Sandusky	12	55
Upper Sandusky	7	62
Tymochtee	8	70
McCutchinville	3	73
TIFFIN	11	84
Fort Seneca	8	92
LOWER SANDUSKY	10	102

(19) COLUMBUS to SANDUSKY CITY.

Cin., Cleveland and Col. R. R.		
To Worthington	9	
Delaware	14	23
Cardington	17	40
Iberia	12	52
Galion	7	59
Crestline	3	62
SHELBY	11	73
Mansfield and Sandusky R. R.		
Plymouth	9	82
New Haven	2	84
Centreville	6	90
Havana	4	94
Pontiac	4	98
Monroeville	4	102
Ladd's	8	110
SANDUSKY	8	118

(20) COLUMBUS to PORTSMOUTH.

To South Bloomfield	17	
Circleville	9	26
CHILLICOTHE	21	47
Waverly	15	62
Piketon	4	66
Lucasville	14	80
PORTSMOUTH	12	92

(21) Cleveland to Columbus.

Via Cin., Cleveland and Col. R. R.

To Rockport	7	
Berea	5	12
Olmstead	3	15
Eaton	7	22
Grafton	3	25
La Grange	4	29
Pittsfield	4	33
Wellington	3	36
Rochester	5	41
New London	6	47
Greenwich	7	54
Shelby	13	67
Crestline	11	78
Galion	3	81
Iberia	7	88
Cardington	12	100
Delaware	17	117
Worthington	14	131
Columbus	9	140

(22) Columbus to Lancaster.

To Grove Port	12	
Lithopolis	5	17
Green Castle	5	22
Lancaster	7	29

(23) Zanesville to Maysville, Ky.

To Putnam	1	
Fultonham	10	11
Somerset	10	21
Rushville	8	29
Lancaster	9	38
Clear Creek	8	46
Tarleton	8	54
Kingston	9	63
Chillicothe	10	73
Bourneville	13	86
Bainbridge	11	97
Rainsboro'	8	105
Hillsboro'	10	115
New Market	6	121
Sugar-tree Ridge	7	128
Scott	7	135
Bentonville	10	145
Aberdeen	10	155
Maysville, Ky.	1	156

(24) Zanesville to Marietta.

To Blue Rock	11	
Rokeby	8	19
McConnellsville	8	27
Beverly	18	45
Waterford	2	47
Lowell	9	56
Marietta	12	68

(25) Zanesville to Wooster.

To Dresden	15	
Adam's Mills	3	18
Roscoe	12	30
Coshocton	1	31
Keene's	7	38
Clark's	8	46
Millersburg	8	54
Holmesville	6	60
Fredericksburg	5	65
Wooster	10	75

(26) Wooster to Warren.

To Smithville	8	
Marshallville	6	14
Chippewa	6	20
New Portage	6	26
Akron	9	35
Middlebury	2	37
Tallmadge	3	40
Brimfield	5	45
Franklin Mills	5	50
Ravenna	6	56
Charlestown	5	61
Parisville	5	66
Newton Falls	5	71
Warren	8	79

(27) Lancaster to Mt. Vernon.

To Pleasantville	9	
New Salem	4	13
Thornville	5	18
Jacksontown	4	22
Newark	8	30
St. Louisville	8	38
Utica	4	42
Homer	5	47
Mount Vernon	11	58

(28) Chillicothe to Pt. Pleasant, Ky.

To Richmond Dale	16	
Jackson	15	31
Rocky Hill	8	39
Thurman	6	45
Rio Grande	6	51
Gallipolis	11	62
Point Pleasant	6	68

(29) Chillicothe to Marietta.

To Gillespieville	15	
Allensville	12	27

McArthurstown	8	35
Lee	14	49
Hobardsville	3	52
Athens	6	58
Amesville	12	70
Bartlett	8	78
Wesley	4	82
Harmer	16	98
MARIETTA	1	99

(30) CHILLICOTHE to MAYSVILLE, KY.

Via West Union.

To Bourneville	13	
Bainbridge	11	24
Cynthiana	5	29
Sinking Spring	10	39
Locust Grove	6	45
Dunbarton	6	51
Dunkinsville	5	56
WEST UNION	5	61
Aberdeen	17	78
MAYSVILLE	1	79

(31) WELLSVILLE to ASHTABULA.

To West Point	7	
New Lisbon	7	14
Franklin Square	5	19
Salem	5	24
Greenford	5	29
Canfield	5	34
Orange	7	41
Ohls Town	4	45
Warren	6	51
Bristolville	11	62
North Bloomfield	5	67
Orwell	6	73
Rome	5	78
Morgan	4	82
Eagleville	5	87
Jefferson	4	91
ASHTABULA	9	100

(32) PAINESVILLE to CANTON.

To Concord	4	
Chardon	7	11
Munson	4	15
Newbury	7	22
Auburn	3	25
Mantua	6	31
Shalersville	5	36
RAVENNA	6	42
Rootstown	5	47
Randolph	5	52
Hartville	6	58
CANTON	11	69

(33) PAINESVILLE to PITTSBURG, PA.

To Concord	4	
Chardon	7	11
Claridon	5	16
Burton	4	20
Parkman	9	29
Nelson	4	33
Windham	4	37
Braceville	5	42
WARREN	7	49
Niles	6	55
Girard	5	60
Youngstown	4	64
POLAND	6	70
Beaver, (see 35)	31	101
PITTSBURG	28	129

(34) CLEVELAND to WHEELING, VA.

Via Wooster.

To Ohio City	1	
Brooklyn	3	4
Parma	3	7
Strongsville	8	15
Brunswick	6	21
Medina	8	29
Guilford	9	38
Old Hickory	4	42
WOOSTER	10	52
Apple Creek	6	58
Mount Eaton	9	67
Deardoff's Mills	9	76
Strasburg	3	79
Canal Dover	5	84
New Philadelphia	3	87
Uhricksville	9	96
Deersville	11	107
Cadiz	12	119
Short Creek	6	125
Harrisville	3	128
Mount Pleasant	5	133
Coleraine	5	138
Martin's Ferry	5	143
WHEELING, VA.	1	144

(35) CLEVELAND to WELLSVILLE.

Cleveland and Pittsburg R. R.

To Newburgh	8	
Gravel Bank		
Bedford	6	14
Macedonia	6	20
Hudson	6	26
Earlville	6	32

Ravenna	6	38
Rootstown	5	43
Atwater	6	49
Lima	4	53
Alliance	5	58
Winchester	5	63
Moultrie	3	66
Bayard	3	69
Rochester	1	70
Hanover	5	75
Brush Run	6	81
Salineville	5	86
Steubenville Road	5	91
Hammonds	3	94
Yellow Cr.	3	97
WELLSVILLE	2	99

(36) CLEVELAND to BUFFALO, N.Y.

Cleveland and Erie R. R.

To Euclid	9	
Wickliffe	5	14
Willoughby	4	18
Mentor	5	23
Painesville	6	29
Perry	6	35
Madison	5	40
Unionville	2	42
Geneva	3	45
Saybrook	5	50
Ashtabula	4	54
Kingsville	6	60
Conneaut	8	68
Springfield	7	75
Girard	5	80
Fairview	5	85
Swanville	3	88
ERIE	7	95

Erie and North East R. R.

Harbor Creek	7	102
North East	8	110
State Line	4	114

Buffalo and State Line R. R.

Quincy	4	118
Westfield	8	126
Centerville	6	132
DUNKIRK	10	142
Silver Creek	10	152
Lagrange	2	154
Evans Center	7	161
18 Mile Creek	7	168
Rodgers Road	5	173
BUFFALO	10	183

(37) CLEVELAND to BUFFALO, N.Y.

Steamboat.

To Fairport	30	
Ashtabula	33	63
Conneaut	14	77
Erie, Pa.	30	107
Dunkirk, N. Y.	48	155
BUFFALO	43	198

(38) CLEVELAND to TOLEDO.

To Ohio City	1	
Rockport	7	8
Dover	5	13
North Ridgeville	7	20
ELYRIA	4	24
Amherst	8	32
Henrietta	3	35
Birmingham	3	38
Florence	3	41
Berlinville	4	45
Milan	8	53
Norwalk	4	57
Monroesville	4	61
Four Corners	3	64
Lyme	3	67
Bellevue	3	70
Green Creek	10	80
LOWER SANDUSKY	8	88
Black Swamp	8	96
Woodville	7	103
Stony Ridge	7	110
Perrysburg	9	119
Maumee City	1	120
TOLEDO	10	130

(39) CLEVELAND to WARREN.

To Warrensville	8	
Barry	5	13
Chagrin Falls	7	20
Bridge Creek	7	27
Auburn	3	30
Welshfield	3	33
Parkman	4	37
Nelson	4	41
Garrettsville	3	44
Windham	3	47
Braceville	5	52
WARREN	7	59

(40) BUCYRUS to MANSFIELD.

To Galion	11	
Riblett's	5	16
Ontario	4	20
MANSFIELD	7	27

(41) SANDUSKY to CINCINNATI.

Mad River and Lake Erie R. R.

To Bellevue	15	
Lodi	9	24
Republic	5	29
Tiffin	9	38
Oregon	11	49
Cary	5	54
Paterson	13	67
Kenton	11	78
Bell Centre	12	90
Richland	2	92
Huntsville	3	95
Bellefontaine	7	102
West Liberty	8	110
Urbana	10	120
SPRINGFIELD	14	134

Little Miami R. R.

Yellow Springs	10	144
Xenia	10	154
Spring Valley	7	161
Claysville	7	168
Waynesville	4	172
Freeport	5	177
Fort Ancient	3	180
Morrow	4	184
Deerfield	5	189
Foster's	4	193
Loveland's	6	199
Polktown	2	201
Germany	2	203
Milford	2	205
Plainville	5	210
Columbia	4	214
CINCINNATI	5	219

(42) SANDUSKY to NEWARK.

Mansfield and Sandusky R. R.

To Ladd's	8	
Monroeville	8	16
Pontiac	4	20
Havana	4	24
Centreville	4	28
New Haven	6	34
Plymouth	2	36
Shelby*	9	45
Spring Mill	6	51
MANSFIELD†	5	56

Columbus and Lake Erie R. R.

Lexington	9	65
Belville	5	70
Independence	6	76
Ankeneytown	5	81
Fredericton	5	86
MOUNT VERNON	6	92
Hunt's	6	98
Gambier	3	101
Utica	4	105
St. Louisville	4	109
Newton	3	112
NEWARK	5	117

* Connects with the Cin. Cleveland and Col. R. R.
To Columbus, (see 19,) 73 miles.
Cleveland, (see 21,) 67 miles.
† Ohio and Penn. to cross here.

(43) SANDUSKY to CHICAGO, ILL.

To Amherstburg, C. W.	52	
DETROIT, MICH	20	72
Fort Gratiot	70	142
Point au Barques	85	227
Thunder Bay	70	297
Presque Island	80	377
Mackinaw	65	442
Beaver Islands	50	492
Manitou Islands	45	537
MILWAUKEE, WIS	150	687
Racine	25	712
Southport	13	725
CHICAGO	57	782

(44) SANDUSKY to BUFFALO, N. Y.

To Huron	14	
CLEVELAND	45	59
Fairport	30	89
Ashtabula	33	122
Conneaut	14	136
Erie, Pa	30	166
Dunkirk, N. Y	48	214
BUFFALO	43	257

(45) BUFFALO, N. Y. to N. YORK.

Attica and Buffalo R. R.

To Lancaster	10	
Alden	10	20
Darien	5	25
ATTICA	6	31

Tonawanda R. R.

Alexander	3	34
Batavia	8	42
Byron	7	49
Bergen	7	56
Churchville	4	60
ROCHESTER	14	74

Auburn and Rochester R. R.

Brighton	4	78
Pittsford	4	82
Victor	12	94
Canandaigua	9	103
Chapinsville	3	106
Short's Mills	3	109
Clifton Springs	5	114
West Vienna	3	117
East Vienna	1	118
Oak's Corners	3	121
GENEVA	5	126
Waterloo	7	133
Seneca Falls	4	137
Cayuga Bridge	5	142
AUBURN	10	152

Auburn and Syracuse R. R.

Sennet	5	157
Skaneateles Junction	4	161
Elbridge	1	162
Camillus	8	170
Geddes	6	176
SYRACUSE	2	178

Syracuse and Utica R. R.

Manlius	10	188
Chittenango	4	192
Canastota	6	198
Wampsville	3	201
Oneida Depot	3	204
Verona Centre	4	208
ROME	9	217
Oriskany	7	224
Whitesboro'	4	228
UTICA	3	231

Utica and Schenectady R. R.

Schuyler	8	239
Herkimer	7	246
Little Falls	6	252
St. Johnsville	10	262
Palatine Church	3	265
Fort Plain	3	268
Palatine Bridge	3	271
Spraker's	3	274
Fonda	8	282
Tribes Hill	6	288
Amsterdam	5	293
Cranesville	4	297
Hoffman's	3	300
SCHENECTADY	9	309

Mohawk and Hudson R. R.

ALBANY	16	325

Steamboat.

NEW YORK	145	470

(46) DUNKIRK, N. Y., to N. YORK.

Via New York and Erie R. R.

To Forestville	8	
Smith's Mills	4	12
Perrysburgh	7	19
Dayton	3	22
Albion	9	31
Little Valley	6	37
Great Valley	11	48
Nine Mile Creek	8	56
Alleghany	4	60
Olean	4	64
Hinsdale	7	71
Cuba	5	76
Friendship	9	85
Belvidere	5	90
Phillipsville	3	93
Scio	4	97
Genesee	4	101
Andover	9	110
Baker's Bridge	8	118
Almond	4	122
HORNELLSVILLE	5	127
Canister	5	132
Cameron	13	145
Rathboneville	7	152
Addison	5	157
Painted Post	10	167
CORNING	2	169
Blossburg, Pa.	40	
Big Flats	8	177
Junction	6	183
ELMIRA	5	188
Millport	12	
Jefferson	9	
Wellsburg	7	195
Chemung	6	201
Factoryville	4	205
Barton	7	212
Smithboro'	2	214
Tioga Centre	4	218
OWEGO	6	224
Campville	7	231
Union	6	237
BINGHAMTON	9	246
Windsor	5	251
Great Bend	9	260
Lanesboro'	9	269
Gulf Summit	8	277
Deposit	8	285
Chehocton	13	298
Stockport	4	302
Equinunk	6	308
Hankins	11	319
Calicoon	7	326

Cohecton	5	331
Narrowsburg	8	339
Mast Hope	6	345
Lackawaxen	6	351
Barryville	4	355
Pond Eddy	7	362
Stairway Brook	2	364
PORT JERVIS	9	373
Shin Hollow	6	379
Otisville	7	386
Howell's	5	391
Middletown	3	394
New Hampton	3	397
GOSHEN	4	401
Chester	5	406
Oxford	3	409
Monroe	2	411
Turner's	3	414
Wilkes'	3	417
Monroe Works	3	420
Sloatsburg	6	426
Ramapo Works	1	427
Sufferns	2	429
Monsey	5	434
Spring Valley	2	436
Clarkstown	2	438
Blauveltville	4	442
Piermont, (town)	4	446
PIERMONT, (pier)	1	447
Steamboat.		
NEW YORK	24	471

(47) WHEELING, VA., to BALTIMORE, PHILADELPHIA, & N. YORK.

Baltimore and Ohio R. R.

To Moundsville	11	
Roseby's Rk.	7	18
Cameron	10	28
Welling Tunnel	2	30
Bellton	6	36
Br'd Tree	3	39
Littleton	3	42
Burton	7	49
Glover's Gap	4	53
Mannington	7	60
Farmington	7	67
Barrackville	5	72
FAIRMOUNT	5	77
Benton's Ferry	4	81
Nazum's Mills	8	89
Valley Falls	2	91
Fetterman	6	97
Thornton	8	105
Independence	6	111
Simpson's	2	113
Tunnelton	6	119
Rolesbury	7	126
Cr. Summit	9	137
Oakland	10	147
Altamount	9	156
Frankville	7	163
Bloomington	8	171
Piedmont	2	173
New Creek	5	178
Rawlin's Sta.	10	188
Brady's Mill	6	194
CUMBERLAND	7	201
Patterson's Creek	8	209
Green Spring Run	6	215
Little Cacapon	7	222
No. 12 Water Station	7	229
Rockwell's Run	11	240
Bruce's Dep.	7	247
Sir John's Run	4	251
Hancock	5	256
Cherry Run	10	266
N. Mountain	6	272
Martinsburg	6	278
Kearneysville	9	287
Duffield's	5	292
HARPER'S FERRY	6	298
Sandy Hook	1	299
Berlin	5	304
Point of Rocks	6	310
Buckeystone	7	317
Monocacy	4	321
Ijamsville	5	326
Monrovia	4	330
Plane No. 4	4	334
Mount Airy	2	336
Plane No. 1	3	339
Gaithers	8	347
Sykesville	1	348
Marriottsville	4	352
Woodstock	3	355
Elysville	4	359
Ellicott's Mill	6	365
Relay House	6	371
Mount Clare	7	378
BALTIMORE	2	380

Philadelphia, Wilmington, and Baltimore R. R.

Canton	3	383
Stemmer's Run	7	390
Chase's	6	396
Gunpowder	4	400
Perryman's	8	408
Hall's Cross Roads	4	412
Havre de Grace	5	417

Cecil	1	418
Charlestown	5	423
North East	3	426
Elktown	6	432
Newark, Del	6	438
Stanton	6	444
Newport	2	446
WILMINGTON	4	450
Naaman's Creek	8	458
Marcus' Hook, Pa.	2	460
Chester	3	463
Lazaretto	4	467
Gray's Ferry	7	474
PHILADELPHIA	3	477
Philadelphia and Trenton R. R.		
Philadelphia Depot	2	479
Tacony	7	486
Cornwell's	5	491
Andalusia	2	493
Bristol	4	497
Morrisville	9	506
New Brunswick & Trenton R. R.		
TRENTON	1	507
Princeton	10	517
Kingston	4	521
Dean's Pond	4	525
NEW BRUNSWICK	9	534
New Jersey R. R.		
Metuchin	5	539
Rahway	7	546
Elizabethtown	6	552
NEWARK	5	557
Jersey City	8	565
Steamboat.		
NEW YORK	1	566

(48) PITTSBURG to PHILADELPHIA.

Penn. Central R. R.

To Liberty		
Irwin's		
Radebaughs		
Latrobe		40
Derry	9	49
Blairsville Junction	9	58
Lockport	7	65
New Florence	5	70
Ninevah	5	75
Johnstown	10	85
Conemaugh	2	87
Half Way House	8	95
Jefferson	4	99
Summit	10	109
HOLLIDAYSBURG	10	119
Altoona	6	125
Fastoria	8	133
Spruce Creek	13	146
Petersburg	6	152
HUNTINGTON	7	159
Mill Creek	5	164
Mount Union	6	170
Hamilton	3	173
McVeytown	10	183
Andersons	5	188
Lewiston	7	195
Mifflintown	12	207
Perryville	3	210
Tuscarora	6	216
Millerstown	7	223
Newport	6	229
Baileys	4	233
Aqueduct	5	238
Duncannon	3	241
Rockville	9	250
HARRISBURG	6	256
Harrisburg and Lancaster R. R.		
High Spire	6	262
Middletown	4	266
Elizabethtown	9	275
Mount Joy	6	281
Dillerville	11	292
LANCASTER	1	293
Columbia & Philadelphia R. R.		
Enterprise	7	300
Paradise	3	303
Kinzies	4	307
Penningtonville	7	314
Parkesburg	3	317
Coatesville	5	322
Downington	7	329
Whiteland	4	333
Paoli	6	339
Westchester Turnout	3	342
Morgan's Corner	7	349
White Hall	3	352
Head of Inclined Plane	7	359
PHILADELPHIA	4	363

MICHIGAN.

(49) DETROIT to NEW BUFFALO.

Central Railroad.

To Dearbornville	10	
Wayne	7	17
Ypsilanti	12	29
Geddes' Mills	4	33
ANN ARBOR	4	37
Delhi	6	43
Scio	2	45

Dexter	2	47
Davison's	9	56
Franciscoville	6	62
Grass Lake	3	65
Leoni	3	68
JACKSON	7	75
Barry	5	80
Gidley's Station	5	85
Albion	11	96
Marengo	7	103
Marshall	6	109
Ceresco	5	114
Battle Creek	8	122
Charleston	10	132
Galesburg	4	136
Comstock	4	140
KALAMAZOO	4	144
Paw Paw Station	16	160
Decatur	8	168
Dowagiac	10	178
Pokagon	6	184
Niles	7	191
Buchanan	5	196
Terre Coupee	6	202
New Buffalo	16	218
MICHIGAN CITY	10	228
Porter	12	240
Lake	8	248
Gibson's	10	258
Junction	10	268
3 Mile Side Track		
CHICAGO	10	278

(51) DETROIT to LANSING.

To Redford	15	
Livonia	3	18
Farmington	4	22
Novi	5	27
Kensington	10	37
Brighton	7	44
Genoa	5	49
Howell	5	54
Cedar	7	61
Conway	6	67
Phelpstown	9	76
Williamstown	7	83
LANSING	7	90

(52) DETROIT to LANSING.

To Jackson, (see 49)	77	
LANSING, (see 64)	40	117

(53) DETROIT to PORT HURON.

To Roseville	9	
Mount Clemens	13	22
New Haven	7	29
Columbus	11	40
St. Clair	11	51
PORT HURON	12	63

(54) DETROIT to PONTIAC.

Detroit and Pontiac R. R.

To Royal Oak	12	
Birmingham	6	18
PONTIAC	7	25

(55) DETROIT to SAGINAW.

To Pontiac, (see 54)	25	
Waterford	5	30
Austin	3	33
Clarkson	3	36
Springfield	3	39
Groveland	7	46
Stony Run	5	51
Grand Blanc	4	55
FLINT	8	63
Genesee	4	67
Thetford	7	74
Bridgeport	13	87
SAGINAW	11	98

(56) PONTIAC to OWASSO.

To Waterford Centre	5	
East White Lake	5	10
White Lake	4	14
Rose	6	20
Fentonville	8	28
Argentine	9	37
Byron	5	42
Vernon	6	48
Shiawasse	5	53
Corunna	5	58
OWASSO	4	62

(57) MONROE to CHICAGO, ILL.

Via Southern Railroad.

To Ida	12	
Petersburg	8	20
Deerfield	4	24
ADRIAN*	14	38
Clayton	11	49
Hudson	6	55
Oseco	12	67
HILLSDALE	5	72
Jonesville	5	77
County Line	9	86
COLD WATER	9	95

Bronson's Prairie	13	108
Fawn River	10	114
Sturgis†	4	118
White Pigeon	12	130
Bristol, Ia.	7	137
Elkhart	11	148
Mishawaka	9	157
SOUTH BEND‡	4	161
Terre Coupee	9	170
LA PORTE	18	188
Holmesville	9	197
Calumet	9	206
Baily Town	3	209
Millers	8	217
Ainsworth	17	234
CHICAGO	12	246

(58) MONROE to ANN ARBOR.

To East Raisinville	9	
North Raisinville	3	12
London	3	15
Milan	4	19
York	4	23
Saline	6	29
Lodi	3	32
ANN ARBOR	6	38

(59) ADRIAN to TOLEDO, O.

Erie and Kalamazoo R. R.

To Palmyra	6	
Blissfield	4	10
Ottawa Lake	8	18
Sylvania	3	21
TOLEDO	12	33

(60) ADRIAN to YPSILANTI.

To Raisin	4	
Tecumseh	6	10
Clinton	5	15
Benton	7	22
Saline	5	27
Pittsfield	5	32
YPSILANTI	5	37

(61) LANSING to GRAND HAVEN.

To Delta	6	
Eagle	7	13
Portland	10	23
Maple	5	28
Lyons	5	33
IONIA	7	40
Avon	10	50
Flat River	7	57
Ada	8	65
GRAND RAPIDS	10	75
Grandville	7	82
Tallmadge	10	92
Crockery Creek	8	100
GRAND HAVEN	9	109

(62) LANSING to DEXTER.

To Delhi Centre	7	
Alaiedon	4	11
Mason	4	15
Ingham	9	24
Stockbridge	9	33
Unadilla	6	39
DEXTER	13	52

(63) LANSING to PONTIAC.

To Williamstown	7	
Phelpstown	7	14
Conway	9	23
Cedar	6	29
HOWELL	7	36
Osceola Centre	5	41
Hartland	5	46
Highland	7	53
Milford	4	57
Commerce	6	63
Waterford Centre	5	68
PONTIAC	5	73

(64) LANSING to JACKSON.

To Delhi Centre	7	
Alaiedon	5	12
Mason	4	16
Eden	5	21
Aurelius	5	26
West Rives	5	31
JACKSON	9	40

(65) JACKSON to TOLEDO, O.

To Michigan Centre	5	
Napoleon	6	11
Norvell	4	15
Elba	3	18
Manchester	4	22
Clinton	7	29
Tecumseh	5	34
Raisin	6	40
ADRIAN	4	44
Erie and Kalamazoo R. R.		
TOLEDO, (see 59)	33	77

(66) JACKSON to JONESVILLE.

To Spring Arbor	10	
Concord	4	14
Scipio Centre	9	23
JONESVILLE	4	27

(67) MARSHALL to COLDWATER.

To Tekonsha	13	
Girard	5	18
COLDWATER	6	24

(68) MARSHALL to CENTREVILLE.

To Tekonsha	13	
Burlington	5	18
Union City	4	22
Sherwood	7	29
Fort Pleasant	7	36
Nottoway	6	42
CENTREVILLE	5	47

(69) BATTLE CREEK to GRAND RAPIDS.

To Bedford	6	
Johnstown	6	12
Hastings	12	24
GRAND RAPIDS	32	56

(70) KALAMAZOO to MOTTVILLE.

To Schoolcraft	14	
Flowerfield	5	19
Three Rivers	8	27
Constantine	9	36
MOTTVILLE	6	42

(71) KALAMAZOO to SAUGATUCK.

To Cooper	6	
Plainwell	5	11
Otsego	4	15
Allegan	11	26
Manlius	10	36
SAUGATUCK	14	50

(72) KALAMAZOO to ST. JOSEPH.

To Paw Paw Station	18	
Paw Paw	4	22
Hamilton	11	33
Keelersville	4	37
Bainbridge	7	44
ST. JOSEPH	12	56

(73) NILES to ST. JOSEPH.

To Berrien Springs	10	
ST. JOSEPH	15	25

(74) DETROIT to BUFFALO, N. Y.

Steamboat.

To Amherstburg, C. W.	20	
Sandusky, O.	52	72
Huron	14	86
CLEVELAND	45	131
Fairport	30	161
Ashtabula	33	194
Conneaut	14	208
Erie, Pa.	30	238
Dunkirk, N. Y.	48	286
BUFFALO	43	329

(75) DETROIT to CHICAGO, ILL.

Steamboat.

Fort Gratiot	70	
Point au Barques	85	155
Thunder Bay	70	225
Presque Isle	80	305
Mackinaw	65	370
Beaver Islands	50	420
Manitou Islands	45	465
MILWAUKEE, WIS.	150	615
Racine	25	640
Southport	13	653
CHICAGO	57	710

(76) DETROIT to FORT WILKINS.

(*On Lake Superior.*)

Steamboat.

To Fort Gratiot	70	
Point au Barques	85	155
Thunder Bay	70	225
Presque Isle	80	305
Sault St. Marie	100	405
White Fish Point	40	445
Hurricane River	40	485
Pictured Rocks	35	520
FORT WILKINS and Copper Harbor	120	640

(77) GRAND HAVEN to MILWAUKEE.

Steamboat.

To MILWAUKEE	90	

(78) NEW BUFFALO to CHICAGO.

Steamboat.

Michigan City, Ia.	10	
City West	13	23
CHICAGO, ILL.	33	56

INDIANA.

(79) INDIANAPOLIS to CINCINNATI, OHIO.

Via Rushville.

To Sugar Creek	15	
Kinder	5	20
Morristown	6	26
Beech Grove	7	33
Rushville	7	40

New Salem	7	47
Andersonville	4	51
Laurel	6	57
Metamora	5	62
Brookville	7	69
Cedar Grove	8	77
New Trenton	5	82
Harrison, O.	6	88
Clark's Store	4	92
Miami	4	96
Cheviot	6	102
CINCINNATI	7	109

(80) INDIANAPOLIS to CINCINNATI.

Via Shelbyville.

To Pleasantview	14	
Brandywine	6	20
SHELBYVILLE	6	26
Coon's Creek	8	34
St. Omer	3	37
Greensburg	10	47
Napoleon	12	59
Delaware	6	65
North Hogan	5	70
Manchester	7	77
LAWRENCEBURG	10	87
Elizabethtown, O.	6	93
Cleves	3	96
Dry Ridge	5	101
Cheviot	4	105
CINCINNATI	7	112

(81) INDIANAPOLIS to MADISON.

Madison and Indianapolis R. R.

To Southport	6	
Greenwood	4	10
Franklin	10	20
Amity	5	25
Edinburg	5	30
Taylorsville	5	35
COLUMBUS	6	41
Elizabethtown	7	48
Scipio	7	55
Queensville	3	58
Vernon	6	64
Butler's Switch	2	66
Champion's Mill	4	70
Dupont	2	72
Big Creek	2	74
Middlefork	2	76
Wert	4	80
MADISON	6	86

(82) INDIANAPOLIS to LOUISVILLE.

To Edinburg, (see 81)...... 30

Jeffersonville R. R.

Taylorsville	5	35
COLUMBUS	6	41
Bannerville	7	48
Jonesville	3	51
Rockford	5	56
Farmington	6	62
Langdons	4	66
Baker's Mill	4	70
Center Switch	4	74
Vienna	6	80
Henryville	8	88
Memphis	4	92
Sellersburg	6	98
JEFFERSONVILLE	9	107
LOUISVILLE	1	108

(83) INDIANAPOLIS to TERRE HAUTE.

Terre Haute and Richmond R. R.

To Bridgeport	9	
Plainfield	5	14
Cantersburg	3	17
North Belleville	2	19
Claysville	2	21
Morristown	4	25
Crittenden	2	27
Coatsville	2	29
Fillmore	4	33
Greencastle	6	39
Hendricks	5	44
Reel's Mill	4	48
Croy's Creek	4	52
Brazil	5	57
Highland	4	61
Cloverland	2	63
Woods Mills	2	65
TERRE HAUTE	8	73

(84) NEW ALBANY to JULIET.

New Albany and Salem R. R.

To Bennetsville	10	
New Providence	9	19
Pekin	5	24
Harristown	6	30
Salem	5	35
Buena Vista	10	45
Orleans	12	57
JULIET	8	65

(86) INDIANAPOLIS to ST. LOUIS, Mo.

To Terre Haute, (see 85) ...75
Livingston, Ill. 13 88
Marshall 4 92
Martinsville......12 104
Casey 6 110
Greenup......10 120
Woodbury......7 127
Tentopolis......10 137
Ewington 9 146
Freemanton......5 151
Howard's Point 9 160
Cumberland 7 167
VANDALIA 6 173
Mulberry Grove 9 182
Greenville 8 190
Hickory Grove 9 199
Highland 14 213
Troy......6 219
Collinsville......6 225
ST. LOUIS, Mo......15 240

(87) INDIANAPOLIS to SPRINGFIELD, ILL.

To TERRE HAUTE, (see 85). 75
Elbridge, Ill. 10 85
Paris 10 95
Grandview......12 107
Hitesville 6 113
Charleston 12 125
Bethsaida......8 133
Paradise 7 140
Cochran's Grove 8 148
SHELBYVILLE 12 160
Taylorsville 35 195
Rochester 16 211
SPRINGFIELD 9 220

(88) INDIANAPOLIS to MONTEZUMA.

To Hampton......12
Danville 8 20
New Winchester 7 27
New Maysville 5 32
Bainbridge......6 38
Portland Mills......14 52
Rockville 13 65
MONTEZUMA 10 75

(89) INDIANAPOLIS to COVINGTON.

To Clermont 8
Brownsburg 6 14
Jamestown 14 28
New Ross 7 35
CRAWFORDSVILLE 10 45
Waynetown 10 55
Hillsboro' 6 61
Coles' Creek 5 66
COVINGTON 8 74

(90) INDIANAPOLIS to WILLIAMSPORT.

To Crawfordsville, (see 89) .45
Pleasant Hill 13 58
Newtown 5 63
Rob Roy 6 69
Attica 4 73
WILLIAMSPORT 2 75

(91) INDIANAPOLIS to LA FAYETTE.

To Crawfordsville, (see 89) .45
Romney 15 60
LA FAYETTE......11 71

(92) INDIANAPOLIS to LA FAYETTE.

To Piketon 9
Royalton......5 14
Thornleyville 5 19
Lebanon 6 25
Thornton 10 35
Frankfort 12 47
Jefferson......4 51
Prairieville......6 57
Monroe 5 62
Wyandotte......5 67
Dayton 5 72
LA FAYETTE......7 79

(93) INDIANAPOLIS to NILES, MICH.

To Augusta......9
Eagle Village 6 15
Northfield 5 20
Kirk's Cross Roads 12 32
Michigantown......10 42
Middlefork 6 48
Burlington......5 53
Carroll......10 63
LOGANSPORT......8 71
Metea 12 83
Rochester......11 94
Sidney 13 107
Plymouth......10 117
South Bend......24 141
Bertrand, Mich. 8 149
NILES 4 153

(94) INDIANAPOLIS to GREENVILLE, O.

To Allisonville	11	
Noblesville	11	22
Strawtown	7	29
Anderson	17	46
Chesterfield	5	51
Yorktown	6	57
Muncietown	8	65
Smithfield	7	72
Windsor	6	78
Macksville	4	82
Winchester	6	88
Randolph	7	95
Dark, O.	5	100
GREENVILLE	10	110

(95) INDIANAPOLIS to COLUMBUS, O.

To Cumberland	10	
Philadelphia	5	15
Greenfield	5	20
Kinnard	4	24
Charlotteville	4	28
Knightstown	5	33
Lewisville	10	43
Dublin	8	51
Cambridge	2	53
Centreville	9	62
Richmond	6	68
New Westerville, O.	6	74
Eaton	10	84
West Alexandria	6	90
Medill	6	96
Liberty	7	103
DAYTON	7	110
Fairfield	11	121
Enon	7	128
Springfield	7	135
Vienna	10	145
Summerford	5	150
La Fayette	5	155
West Jefferson	8	163
Alton	5	168
COLUMBUS	9	177

(96) BROOKVILLE to CAMBRIDGE.

To Blooming Grove	7	
Everton	4	11
Connersville	6	17
Milton	10	27
CAMBRIDGE	2	29

(97) LAWRENCEBURG to MADISON.

To Aurora	4	
Rising Sun	8	12
Grant's Creek	4	16
Patriot	6	22
Florence	7	29
Vevay	9	38
Morefield	6	44
Home	5	49
MADISON	10	59

(98) MADISON to LOUISVILLE, KY.

To South Hanover	5	
Saluda	6	11
New Washington	7	18
Charleston	11	29
Utica	8	37
Jeffersonville	9	46
LOUISVILLE	1	47

(99) LOUISVILLE, KY., to VINCENNES.

To Portland	3	
New Albany, Ia.	1	4
Greenville	12	16
Palmyra	9	25
Fredericksburg	5	30
Hardinsburg	5	35
Chambersburg	6	41
Paoli	6	47
Natchez	16	63
Mount Pleasant	12	75
Washington	15	90
Berryville	7	97
VINCENNES	14	111

(100) LOUISVILLE, KY., to ORLEANS.

To Jeffersonville, Ia.	1	
Hamburg	8	9
Bennettsville	8	17
New Providence	5	22
Pekin	3	25
Salem	11	36
Claysville	12	48
ORLEANS	10	58

(101) EDINBURG to RUSHVILLE.

To Shelbyville	17	
Little Blue River	7	24
Manilla	6	30
RUSHVILLE	8	38

(102) MADISON to INDIANAPOLIS.

Madison and Indianapolis R. R.

To Wert	6	
Middlefork	4	10
Big Creek	2	12

Dupont 2 14
Champion's Mill 2 16
Butler's Switch 4 20
Vernon 2 22
Queensville 6 28
Scipio 3 31
Elizabethtown 7 38
COLUMBUS 7 45
Taylorsville 6 51
Edinburg 5 56
Amity 5 61
Franklin 5 66
Greenwood 10 76
Southport 4 80
INDIANAPOLIS 6 86

(103) MADISON to TERRE HAUTE.

To Columbus, (see 102) 45
Lefevre 8 53
Nashville 12 65
Unionville 10 75
BLOOMINGTON 8 83
Whitehall 7 90
Spencer 8 98
VANDALIA 9 107
Bowling Green 8 115
Christie's Prairie 10 125
TERRE HAUTE 14 139

(104) BLOOMINGTON to LA FAYETTE.

To Ellittsville 7
Mount Tabor 6 13
Gosport 3 16
Mill Grove 9 25
Clover Dale 5 30
Putnamville 7 37
Greencastle 5 42
Fincastle 12 54
Parkersburg 7 61
CRAWFORDSVILLE 13 74
Romney 15 89
LA FAYETTE 11 100

(105) MOUTH OF WABASH RIVER to LA FAYETTE.

Steamboat.

To New Harmony 52
Mount Carmel 45 97
VINCENNES 35 132
Russellville 13 145
Palestine 18 163
Merom 5 168
Hutsonville 8 176
York 8 184
Darwin 11 195
TERRE HAUTE 25 220
Clinton 16 236
Montezuma 11 247
Newport Landing 7 254
Perryville 18 272
COVINGTON 8 280
Baltimore 3 283
Portland 8 291
Williamsport 5 296
La Grange 14 310
LA FAYETTE 13 323

(106) EVANSVILLE to TERRE HAUTE.

To Sandersville 10
Princeton 20 30
Patoka 4 34
VINCENNES 20 54
West Union 15 69
Carlisle 8 77
Merom 12 89
Greysville 5 94
Furman's Creek 5 99
Prairie Creek 8 107
Prairieton 7 114
TERRE HAUTE 9 123

(107) TERRE HAUTE to LOGANSPORT.

To Numa 8
Clinton 7 15
Highland 10 25
Newport 6 31
Eugene 7 38
Perryville 7 45
COVINGTON 7 52
Portland 8 60
Rob Roy 5 65
Attica 4 69
Shawnee Prairie 5 74
West Point 8 82
LA FAYETTE 11 93
Americus 11 104
Delphi 7 111
Lockport 9 120
LOGANSPORT 12 132

(108) TERRE HAUTE to CRAWFORDSVILLE.

To Roseville 15
Rockville 9 24
Bruin's Cross Roads 8 32
Waveland 6 38
CRAWFORDSVILLE 14 52

(109) Logansport to Toledo, O.

To Lewisburg	9	
Peru	9	18
Wabash	15	33
La Gro	6	39
Huntington	13	52
Aboite	16	68
Fort Wayne	12	80
New Haven	17	97
Antwerp, O.	7	104
Junction	14	118
Defiance	10	128
Milldale	4	132
Florida	5	137
Napoleon	8	145
Damascus	8	153
Providence	6	159
Waterville	12	171
Maumee City	5	176
Toledo	9	185

(110) Fort Wayne to Cincinnati, Ohio.

To Poughkeepsie	12	
Decatur	12	24
Limber Lost	12	36
Bear Creek	9	45
Jay	8	53
Deerfield	12	65
Winchester	7	72
Lynn	11	83
New Garden	6	89
Chester	5	94
Richmond	5	99
Abington	9	108
Brownsville	6	114
Liberty	5	119
Dunlapsville	5	124
Fairfield	6	130
Brookville	7	137
Cedar Grove	8	145
New Trenton	5	150
Harrison, O.	6	156
Clark's Store	4	160
Miami	4	164
Cheviot	6	170
Cincinnati	7	177

(111) La Porte to Joliet, Ill.

To Door Village	4	
Valparaiso	18	22
Deep River	9	31
Lake Court House	9	40
Endor, Ill.	10	50
Crete	9	59
Chelsea	11	70
Joliet	12	82

(112) Michigan City to Indianapolis.

To La Porte	13	
Plymouth	30	43
Indianapolis, (see 93)	117	160

ILLINOIS.

(113) Springfield to Cincinnati.

To Rochester	9	
Taylorsville	16	25
Shelbyville	35	60
Cochran's Grove	12	72
Paradise	8	80
Bethsaida	7	87
Charleston	8	95
Hitesville	12	107
Grandview	6	113
Paris	12	125
Elbridge	10	135
Terre Haute, Ia.	10	145
Van Buren	12	157
Brazil	7	164
Manhattan	8	172
Green Castle	7	179
Stilesville	13	192
Belleville	8	200
Plainfield	5	205
Bridgeport	6	211
Indianapolis	9	220
Cincinnati, (see 79)	109	329

(114) Springfield to Golconda.

To Zanesville	38	
Hillsboro'	16	54
Hurricane	15	69
Vandalia	12	81
Foster's	13	94
Salem	12	106
Jordan's Prairie	14	120
Mount Vernon	9	129
Spring Garden	11	140
Benton	12	152
Frankfort	7	159
Marion	13	172
Sarahsville	8	180
Golconda	28	208

(115) Springfield to St. Louis.

To Chatham	7	
Auburn	8	15
Carlinville	24	39

Macoupin 6 45
Shipman 8 53
Monticello 14 67
Alton 5 72
St. Louis, Mo. 24 96

(116) Springfield to Naples.

Sangamon and Morgan R. R.

Berlin 17
Island Grove 4 21
Strown's 5 26
Jacksonville 7 33
Jones' 5 38
Bethel 9 47
Vaugundy 5 52
Naples 5 57

(117) Springfield to Quincy.

To Naples, (see 116) 57
Griggsville 10 67
Beverly 10 77
Liberty 14 91
Burton 6 97
Quincy 9 106

(118) Springfield to Keokuck, Iowa.

To Richland 10
Pleasant Plains 6 16
Lancaster 7 23
Virginia 10 33
Beardstown 14 47
Frederickville 4 51
Rushville 8 59
Camden 13 72
Huntsville 6 78
Pulaski 5 83
Augusta 3 86
Plymouth 5 91
St. Mary's 4 95
Elm Tree 7 102
Carthage 7 109
Warsaw 18 127
Keokuck 4 131

(119) Springfield to Burlington, Iowa.

To Rushville, (see 118) 59
Littleton 6 65
Doddsville 6 71
Macomb 13 84
Blandinsville 14 98
Burlington 24 122

(120) Springfield to Lewistown.

To Athens 14
Petersburg 8 22
Sangamon River 12 34
Bath 8 42
Havanna 8 50
Waterford 5 55
Lewistown 5 60

(121) Springfield to Chicago.

To Twelve Mills 8
Middletown 12 20
Delavan 9 29
Dillon 23 52
Tremont 5 57
Groveland 6 63
Peoria 6 69
Chicago, (see 143) 165 234

(122) Springfield to Covington, Ia.

To Mechanicsburg 15
Decatur 24 39
Cerro Gordo 15 54
Monticello 10 64
North Bend 13 77
Urbanna 9 86
Homer 14 100
Danville 20 120
Covington 15 135

(123) Vincennes, Ia., to Shawneetown.

To St. Francisville 10
Armstrong 9 19
Mount Carmel 9 28
Graysville 18 46
Phillipstown 9 55
Carmi 9 64
Emma 8 72
New Haven 6 78
Shawneetown 17 95

(124) Vincennes to St. Louis, Mo.

To Lawrenceville 9
Prairieton 10 19
Olney 13 32
Maysville 16 48
Xenia 16 64
Frederickstown 9 73
Salem 9 82
Carlyle 24 106
Shoal Creek 9 115
Aviston 6 121
Lebanon 11 132
Rock Spring 4 136
Belleville 9 145
French Village 8 153

Wiggins' Ferry	5	158
St. Louis, Mo.	1	159

(125) Vincennes to Alton.

To Carlyle, (see 124)	106	
Shoal Creek	9	115
Highland	8	123
Marine Settlement	12	135
Edwardsville	13	148
Upper Alton	12	160
Alton	2	162

(126) Vincennes to Chicago.

To Russellville	10	
Palestine	15	25
Hutsonville	8	33
York	5	38
Darwin	9	47
Marshall	10	57
Paris	16	73
Bloomfield	13	86
Ridge Farm	10	96
Georgetown	5	101
Danville	10	111
North Fork	15	126
Milford	23	149
Middleport	11	160
Bulbonia's Grove	28	188
Rockville	6	194
Wilmington	12	206
Reed's Grove	7	213
Jackson Creek	4	217
Joliet	7	224
Lockport	6	230
Des Plains	9	239
Summit	10	249
Chicago	13	262

(127) Mt. Carmel to Fairfield.

To Albion	18	
Wabash	9	27
Fairfield	9	36

(128) Salem to Carmi.

To Hickory Hill	18	
Fairfield	21	39
Burnt Prairie	11	50
Carmi	13	63

(129) Salem to Chester.

To Mount Zion	8	
Walnut Hill	5	13
Nashville	19	32
Elkhorn	7	39
Sparta	17	56
Steel's Mill	9	65
Chester	13	78

(130) Shawneetown to Cape Girardeau, Mo.

To Bay	7	
Mount Airy	8	15
Vienna	32	47
Mount Pleasant	10	57
Jonesboro'	12	69
Cedar Creek Landing	18	87
Cape Girardeau	6	93

(131) Shawneetown to St. Louis.

To Equality	14	
Raleigh	12	26
Gallatin	6	32
Benton	20	52
Mount Hawkins	20	72
Nashville	22	94
Akau	14	108
Mascoutah	15	123
Belleville	10	133
French Village	8	141
Wiggins' Ferry	5	146
St. Louis	1	147

(132) Shawneetown to Vandalia.

To Duncantown	23	
McLeansboro'	16	39
Moore's Prairie	13	52
Mount Vernon	14	66
Jordan's Prairie	9	75
Salem	14	89
Foster's	12	101
Vandalia	13	114

(133) Cairo to St. Louis.

Mill Creek	14	
Jonesboro'	20	34
Urbane	12	46
Murpheysboro'	13	59
Jones' Creek	20	79
Chester	8	87
Kaskaskia	7	94
Prairie De Roche	14	108
Waterloo	21	129
Columbia	8	137
St. Louis	15	152

(134) St. Louis, Mo., to Jacksonville.

To Alton	24	
Godfrey	7	31
Delphi	6	37

Jerseyville	8	45
Kane	5	50
Carrollton	8	58
Whitehall	10	68
Manchester	8	76
JACKSONVILLE	17	93

(135) QUINCY to JACKSONVILLE.

To Columbus	15	
Camp Point	6	21
Clayton	6	27
Mount Sterling	12	39
Versailles	9	48
Meredosia	7	55
Bethel	8	63
JACKSONVILLE	12	75

(136) QUINCY to PEORIA.

Via Rushville.

To Columbus	15	
Camp Point	6	21
Clayton	6	27
Mount Sterling	12	39
Ripley	9	48
RUSHVILLE	9	57
Astoria	14	71
Vermont	5	76
Otto	7	83
Lewistown	8	91
Jackson Grove	7	98
Canton	7	105
Farmington	10	115
Trivoli	7	122
PEORIA	18	140

(137) QUINCY to KNOXVILLE.

To Mendon	14	
Woodville	10	24
Chili	3	27
Carthage	14	41
Fountain Green	11	52
MACOMB	17	69
Drowning Fork	5	74
Woodstock	14	88
St. Augustine	3	91
Hartford	7	98
KNOXVILLE	9	107

(138) QUINCY to KEOKUCK, IOWA.

To Ursa	10	
Lima	8	18
Green Plains	8	26
Warsaw	6	32
KEOKUCK	4	36

(139) QUINCY to GALENA.

To Macomb, (see 137)	69	
Swan Creek	16	85
Monmouth	18	103
Spring Grove	7	110
North Henderson	6	116
Pope Creek	6	122
Farlow's Grove	8	130
Pre-emption	5	135
Camden's Mills	10	145
ROCK ISLAND	3	148
Moline	5	153
Hampton	7	160
Port Byron	7	167
Cordova	5	172
Albany	11	183
Fulton	7	190
Savanna	16	206
Hanover	14	220
GALENA	15	235

(140) PEORIA to COVINGTON, IA.

To Groveland	8	
Tremont	6	14
Mackinaw	7	21
Stout's Grove	5	26
Wilksboro'	5	31
Bloomington	10	41
Le Roy	16	57
Santa Anna	10	67
Mahomet	14	81
URBANA	13	94
Homer	14	108
Danville	20	128
COVINGTON	15	143

(141) PEORIA to BURLINGTON, IOWA.

To Kickapoo	11	
Robin's Nest	3	14
Brimfield	5	19
French Creek	6	25
Knoxville	18	43
Galesburg	5	48
Cold Brook	10	58
Monmouth	6	64
Oquawka	18	82
BURLINGTON	16	98

(142) PEORIA to ALBANY.

To Mount Hawley	10	
Wyoming	19	29
Toulon	6	35
Wethersfield	11	46
Burns	17	63

Geneseo	6	69
Crandell's Ferry	15	84
ALBANY	12	96

(143) PEORIA to CHICAGO.

To Chilicothe	18	
Lacon	14	32
Henry	5	37
Hennepin	13	50
Granville	4	54
PERU	10	64
Ottawa	15	79
Marseilles	8	87
Morris	18	105
Dresden	9	114
Channahan	6	120
JOLIET	7	127
Lockport	6	133
Des Plains	9	142
CHICAGO	23	165

(144) PERU to ST. LOUIS, MO.

Steamboat.

To Hennepin	17	
Lacon	18	35
Chilicothe	11	46
Rome	2	48
PEORIA	16	64
Pekin	9	73
Liverpool	25	98
Havanna	9	107
Beardstown	32	139
La Grange	8	147
Meredosia	8	155
Naples	7	162
Florence	10	172
Montezuma	5	177
Bridgeport	6	183
Newport	9	192
Gilford	18	210
Mouth of Illinois River	16	226
Grafton	2	228
Alton	18	246
Missouri River	3	249
ST. LOUIS	18	267

(145) PERU to GALENA.

To La Moille	18	
Dixon	25	43
Buffalo Grove	12	55
Elkhorn Grove	8	63
Rock Creek	5	68
Mount Carroll	12	80
Elizabeth	22	102
GALENA	15	117

(146) OTTAWA to ST. CHARLES.

To Dayton	4	
Northville	16	20
Penfield	9	29
Bristol	5	34
Oswego	5	39
Aurora	7	46
Batavia	6	52
ST. CHARLES	4	56

(147) CHICAGO to DETROIT, MICH.

Steamboat.

To Michigan City, Ia.	40	
NEW BUFFALO, MICH.	10	50
Central Railroad.		
Buchanan	21	71
Niles	6	77
Dowagiac	11	88
Decatur	12	100
Paw Paw Station	8	108
KALAMAZOO	16	114
Comstock	4	128
Galesburg	4	132
Charleston	4	136
Battle Creek	10	146
Ceresco	8	154
Marshall	5	159
Marengo	6	165
Albion	7	172
Gidley's Station	11	183
Barry	5	188
JACKSON	5	193
Leoni	7	200
Grass Lake	3	203
Franciscoville	3	206
Davison's	6	212
Dexter	9	221
Scio	2	223
Delhi	2	225
ANN ARBOR	6	231
Geddes' Mills	4	235
Ypsilanti	4	239
Wayne	12	251
Dearbornville	7	258
DETROIT	10	268

(148) CHICAGO to BUFFALO, N. Y.

Steamboat.

To Southport, Wis.	57	
Racine	13	70
MILWAUKEE	25	95
Manitou Islands, Mich.	150	245
Beaver Islands	45	290
Mackinaw	50	340
Presque Isle	65	405

Thunder Bay	80	485
Point au Barques	70	555
Fort Gratiot	85	640
DETROIT	70	710
Amherstburg, C. W.	20	730
Sandusky, Ohio	52	782
Huron	14	796
CLEVELAND	45	841
Fairport	30	871
Ashtabula	33	904
Conneaut	14	918
Erie, Pa.	30	948
Dunkirk, N. Y.	48	996
BUFFALO	43	1039

(149) CHICAGO to GALENA.

Chicago and Galena R. R.

To Noyesville	10	
Cottage Hill	7	17
Babcock's Grove	4	21
Wheatland	4	25
Junction	5	30
St. Charles Branch	5	35
ELGIN	7	42
Gilberts	8	50
Huntley	5	55
Union	7	62
Marengo	4	66
Garden Prairie	6	72
Belvidere	6	78
Cherry Valley	6	84
ROCKFORD	8	92

Stage.

Vanceburg	19	111
Ridott's	5	116
Silver Creek	6	122
Freeport	7	129
Forestville	8	137
Waddam's Grove	2	139
Alida	2	141
White Oak Springs	32	173
Greenvale	5	178
GALENA	5	183

(150) CHICAGO to MILWAUKEE.

To Dutchman's Point	13	
Wheeling	10	23
Half Day	5	28
Libertyville	6	34
Abingdon	4	38
Waukegan	6	44
Otsego	5	49
Southport, Wis.	12	61
Racine	10	71
Oak Creek	14	85
MILWAUKEE	9	94

(151) CHICAGO to OTTAWA.

Via Plainfield.

To Lyons	13	
Flag Creek	5	18
Cass	5	23
Plainfield	18	41
Ausable	13	54
Lisbon	10	64
Holderman's Grove	4	68
OTTAWA	18	86

(152) CHICAGO to DIXON.

To St. Charles Br., (see 149)	35	
St. Charles	4	39
Sugar Grove	13	52
Acasto	7	59
Little Rock	3	62
Somonauk	6	68
Shabboney's Grove	9	77
Paw Paw Grove	7	84
Mallugin Grove	9	93
Lee Centre	8	101
DIXON	15	116

(153) DIXON to BELOIT, WIS.

To Grand de Tour	6	
Oregon	9	15
Byron	11	26
Kishwaukee	10	36
ROCKFORD	6	42
Harlem	7	49
Roscoe	4	53
Rockton	4	57
BELOIT	3	60

MISSOURI.

(154) ST. LOUIS to NEW ORLEANS.

Steamboat.

Jefferson Barracks, Mo.	9	
Harrisonville, Ill.	19	28
Herculaneum, Mo.	2	30
Selma, Mo.	4	34
St. Genevieve, Mo.	25	59
Chester, Ill.	16	75
Bainbridge, Mo.	45	120
Cape Girardeau, Mo.	12	132
Commerce, Mo.	12	144
CAIRO, ILL, (mouth of Ohio River)	28	172
Columbus, Ky.	18	190
Hickman, Ky.	15	205
New Madrid, Mo.	42	247

Little Prairie, Mo.	30	277
Obion River, Tenn.	29	306
Ashport, Tenn.	8	314
Osceola, Ark.	12	326
Fulton, Tenn.	10	336
Randolph, Tenn., (mouth of Hatchie River)	11	347
Greenock, Ark.	33	380
Memphis, Tenn.	34	414
Commerce, Ark.	27	441
Peyton, Miss.	33	474
Sterling, Ark., (mouth of St. Francis River)	12	486
HELENA, ARK.	10	496
Delta, Miss.	10	506
Victoria, Miss.	65	571
Montgomery's Point, Ark.	1	572
Napoleon, Ark., (mouth of Arkansas River)	20	592
Bolivar Court House, Miss.	12	604
Columbia, Ark.	53	657
Princeton, Miss.	45	702
Providence, La.	29	731
Yazoo River, Miss.	61	792
VICKSBURG, MISS.	12	804
Warrenton, Miss.	10	814
Carthage, La.	19	833
GRAND GULF, MISS.	27	860
Bruinsburg, Miss.	10	870
Rodney, Miss.	10	880
NATCHEZ, MISS.	31	911
Ellis Cliffs, Miss.	18	929
Homochitta River, Miss.	26	955
Fort Adams, Miss.	10	965
Red River Island, La.	11	976
Point Coupee, La. / St. Francisville, La.	60	1036
Port Hudson	11	1047
BATON ROUGE, LA.	25	1072
Plaquemine, La.	23	1095
Donaldsonville, La	34	1129
Jefferson College, La.	19	1148
Red Church, La.	38	1186
Carrollton, La.	20	1206
La Fayette, La.	4	1210
NEW ORLEANS, LA.	2	1212

(155) ST. LOUIS to FALLS OF ST. ANTHONY.

Steamboat.

To Missouri River.	18	
Alton, Ill.	3	21
Grafton, Ill.	18	39
Illinois River, Ill.	2	41
Gilead, Ill.	32	73
Hamburg, Ill.	16	[illegible]
Clarksville, Mo.	15	[illegible]
Louisiana, Mo.	11	107
Hannibal, Mo.	25	132
QUINCY, ILL.	18	150
La Grange, Mo.	10	160
Tully, Mo.	7	167
Warsaw, Ill. / Des Moines River	17	184
Keokuck, Iowa	4	188
Montrose, Iowa / Nauvoo, Ill.	12	200
Madison, Iowa	10	210
BURLINGTON, IOWA	20	230
Oquawka, Ill.	17	247
New Boston, Ill.	19	266
Iowa River, Iowa	1	267
Muscatine, Iowa	25	292
Fairport, Iowa	7	299
Andalusia, Ill.	10	309
Rock Island, Ill. / Davenport, Iowa	9	318
Hampton, Ill.	11	329
Parkhurst, Iowa	8	337
Albany, Ill	19	356
Lyons, Iowa	9	365
Charleston, Iowa	15	380
Savannah, Ill	2	382
Belleview, Iowa	19	401
Fever River, Ill., (to Galena 6 miles)	7	408
DUBUQUE, IOWA	20	428
Peru, Iowa	8	436
Cassville, Wis.	23	459
Gottenburg, Iowa	6	465
Wisconsin River	20	485
Fort Crawford	2	487
Prairie du Chien	2	489
Upper Iowa River	38	527
Bad Axe River	12	539
Root River	23	562
Black River	12	574
Chippewa River	68	642
Maiden's Rock / Lake Pepin	25	667
St. Croix River	35	702
ST. PAUL	26	728
Mendota / Fort Snelling	5	733
ST. ANTHONY	7	740

(156) ST. LOUIS to COUNCIL BLUFFS.

Steamboat.

To mouth of Missouri River	18	
ST. CHARLES	24	42

Missouriton	21	63
Newport	26	89
Griswold City	8	97
Hermann	16	113
Portland	17	130
Cote Sans Dessein	20	150
JEFFERSON CITY	10	160
Marion	17	177
Nashville	10	187
Rocheport	13	200
Boonville	11	211
Arrow Rock	15	226
Glasgow	12	238
Chariton	3	241
Grand River	20	261
Reedsburg	23	284
Lexington	27	311
Camden	17	328
Sibley	16	344
Livingston	17	361
Kansas River	20	381
Parksville	8	389
Platte River	2	391
FORT LEAVENWORTH	20	411
Weston	7	418
St. Joseph	60	478
Noddaway River	14	492
Wolf River	16	508
Great Nemahaw River	18	526
Nishnebotna River	25	551
Little Nemahaw River	12	563
Platte River	70	633
Bellevue Trading House	12	645
COUNCIL BLUFFS	40	685

(157) ST. LOUIS to KEOKUCK, IOWA.

To Waltonham	9	
Feefee	6	15
ST. CHARLES	5	20
Wellsburg	16	36
Flint Hill	7	43
Troy	10	53
Auburn	12	65
Prairieville	10	75
Bowling Green	10	85
Frankfort	14	99
New London	8	107
Hannibal	8	115
PALMYRA	13	128
La Grange	20	148
Tully	7	155
Alexandria	20	175
KEOKUCK, IOWA	4	179

(158) ST. LOUIS to LITTLE ROCK, ARK.

Carondelet	5	
Jefferson Barracks	4	9
Oakville	5	14
Sulphur Springs	8	22
Herculaneum	9	31
Hillsboro'	11	42
Glenfinlay	10	52
Old Mines	10	62
Potosi	7	69
Caledonia	12	81
Iron Mountain	10	91
Farmington	14	105
Mine La Motte	5	110
Fredericktown	12	122
Greenville	35	157
Cane Creek	18	175
Hicks' Ferry, Ark	32	207
Fourche Dumas	15	222
Pocahontas	8	230
Jackson	15	245
Smithville	14	259
Reed's Creek	12	271
Batesville	24	295
Rock Point	11	306
Searcy Court House	32	338
Oakland Grove	25	363
LITTLE ROCK	30	393

(159) ST. LOUIS to NEW MADRID.

To Carondelet	5	
Jefferson Barracks	4	9
Oakville	5	14
Sulphur Springs	8	22
Clifton	5	27
Herculaneum	4	31
Selma	8	39
Rush Tower	8	47
St. Genevieve	14	61
St. Mary's Landing	12	73
Perryville	12	85
Apple Creek	12	97
JACKSON	16	113
Cape Girardeau	11	124
Benton	16	140
Pleasant Plains	10	150
Ogden	8	158
NEW MADRID	23	181

(160) ST. LOUIS to FORT LEAVENWORTH.

To Waltonham	9	
Feefee	6	15
ST. CHARLES	5	20

Cottleville	12	32
Naylor's Store	3	35
Hickory Grove	13	48
Warrenton	10	58
High Hill	9	67
Danville	18	85
Williamsburg	10	95
Jones' Tan Yard	7	102
FULTON	8	110
Millersburg	12	122
Columbia	12	134
Rocheport	13	147
Fayette	15	162
GLASGOW	11	173
FORT LEAVENWORTH, (see 167)	149	322

(161) ST. LOUIS to JEFFERSON CITY.

Via St. Charles.

To Fulton, (see 694)	110	
New Bloomfield	11	121
Hibernia	10	131
JEFFERSON CITY	1	132

(162) ST. LOUIS to JEFFERSON CITY.

Via Mt. Sterling.

To Rock Hill	8	
Manchester	11	19
Fox Creek	14	33
Union	22	55
Adamsburg	23	78
Mount Sterling	14	92
Lynn	16	108
Lisle	8	116
JEFFERSON CITY	10	126

(163) JEFFERSON CITY to INDEPENDENCE.

To Marion	15	
Moniteau	5	20
Midway	9	29
Clark's Fork	6	35
BOONEVILLE	10	45
La Mine	10	55
Arrow Rock	12	67
Marshall	15	82
Mount Hope	25	107
Dover	7	114
Lexington	11	125
Wellington	12	137
Fort Osage	16	153
INDEPENDENCE	12	165

(164) JEFFERSON CITY to FORT LEAVENWORTH.

To Booneville, (see 163)	45	
Franklin	4	49
Fayette	10	59
Glasgow	11	70
FORT LEAVENWORTH, (see 167)	149	219

(165) JEFFERSON CITY to FORT SMITH, ARK.

To High Point	15	
Versailles	25	40
Cole Camp	24	64
WARSAW	16	80
Rocky Ridge	13	93
Judah's Gap	8	101
Elkton	9	110
Bolivar	18	128
Richland	18	146
SPRINGFIELD	12	158
Crane Creek	27	185
McDonald	16	201
Washbourn's Prairie	17	218
Bentonville, Ark.	22	240
Fayetteville	28	268
Boonsboro'	18	286
Evansville	11	297
Natural Dam	12	309
Van Buren	14	323
FORT SMITH	7	330

(166) JEFFERSON CITY to CAPE GIRARDEAU.

To Westphalia	9	
Mavais	17	26
Kinderhook	10	36
Spanish Prairie	12	48
Maramec	15	63
Steelville	12	75
Osage	12	87
Harmony	15	102
CALEDONIA	15	117
Iron Mountain	10	127
Farmington	14	141
Mine La Motte	5	146
Fredericktown	12	158
Paton	24	182
Jackson	14	196
CAPE GIRARDEAU	11	207

(167) GLASGOW to FORT LEAVENWORTH.

To Keytesville	18	
Brunswick	11	29

Pleasant Park	10	39
Dewitt	6	45
Carrollton	7	52
Round Grove	13	65
Richmond	14	79
Crab Orchard	9	88
Liberty	20	108
Barry	10	118
Platte City	15	133
Weston	9	142
FORT LEAVENWORTH	7	149

(168) GLASGOW to HANNIBAL.

To Roanoke	12	
Mount Airy	6	18
Huntsville	6	24
Milton	12	36
Madison	7	43
Paris	12	55
Somerset	12	67
Sharpsburg	7	74
Hydesburg	14	88
HANNIBAL	9	97

(169) MARAMEC to SPRINGFIELD.

To Little Prairie	10	
Little Piney	20	30
Pine Bluff	8	38
Waynesville	12	50
Bellefonte	11	61
Oakland	13	74
Cave Spring	12	86
Woodbury	16	102
Pleasant Prairie	12	114
Walnut Forest	13	127
SPRINGFIELD	8	135

IOWA.

(170) IOWA CITY to KEOKUCK.

To Washington	30	
Fairfield	26	56
Keosauqua	24	80
Bentonsport	10	90
Farmington	8	98
KEOKUCK	32	130

(171) IOWA CITY to MUSCATINE.

To West Liberty	14	
Overman's Ferry	10	24
MUSCATINE	11	35

(172) KEOKUCK to BURLINGTON.

To Montrose	12	
Fort Madison	12	24
Augusta	11	35
BURLINGTON	10	45

(173) FORT MADISON to FARMINGTON.

To West Point	10	
Tuscarora	8	18
FARMINGTON	11	29

(174) BURLINGTON to FORT DES MOINES.

To Hartford	18	
Mount Pleasant	9	27
Rome	8	35
Fairfield	16	51
Ottumwa	25	76
Eddyville	16	92
Oskaloosa	13	105
Red Rock	29	134
FORT DES MOINES	31	165

(175) BURLINGTON to MUSCATINE.

To Yellow Springs	15	
Linton	9	24
Wapello	7	31
Grandview	9	40
MUSCATINE	14	54

(176) MUSCATINE to DAVENPORT.

To Fairport	7	
West Buffalo	11	18
Rockingham	8	26
DAVENPORT	4	30

(177) DAVENPORT to DUBUQUE.

To Dewitt	19	
Maquoketa	22	41
Andrew	7	48
La Motte	14	62
DUBUQUE	12	74

(178) DAVENPORT to DUBUQUE.

To Berlin	16	
Princeton	6	22
Camanche	8	30
Lyons	10	40
Elk River	10	50
Bellevue	24	74
Tete des Motte	10	84
DUBUQUE	12	96

WISCONSIN.

(179) MADISON to GALENA, ILL.

To Middleton	8	
Blue Mound	14	22
Ridgeway	9	31
Dodgeville	9	40
Mineral Point	8	48
Belmont	13	61
Platteville	7	68
Benton	12	80
Hazel Green	5	85
GALENA, ILL.	11	96

(180) MADISON to ROCKFORD, ILL.

To Fitchburg	11	
Rutland	6	17
Union	5	22
Osborn	5	27
Warren	3	30
Janesville	11	41
Rock Valley	7	48
BELOIT	6	54
Rockton	3	57
Roscoe	4	61
Harlem	4	65
ROCKFORD	7	72

(181) MADISON to MILWAUKEE.

Cottage Grove	8	
Deerfield	8	16
Lake Mills	9	25
Aztalan	3	28
Watertown	10	38
Ixonia	8	46
Summit	8	54
Delafield	4	58
Howard	7	65
Waukesha	3	68
Brookfield	5	73
Wawatosa	6	79
MILWAUKEE	5	84

(182) MADISON to GREEN BAY.

To Windsor	11	
Lowville	14	25
Wyocena	9	34
FORT WINNEBAGO	8	42
Rock Hill	17	59
Kingston	2	61
Grand Prairie	4	65
Tichora	5	70
Green Lake	6	76
Rosendale	14	90
FOND DU LAC	13	103
Taycheda	3	106
Calumet Village	10	116
Pequot	3	119
Stockbridge	8	127
Bridgeport	18	145
GREEN BAY	17	162

(183) MILWAUKEE to CHICAGO, ILL.

To Oak Creek	9	
Racine	14	23
Southport	10	33
Otsego, Ill.	12	45
Waukegan	5	50
Abingdon	6	56
Libertyville	4	60
Half Day	6	66
Wheeling	5	71
Dutchman's Point	10	81
CHICAGO	13	94

(184) MILWAUKEE to JANESVILLE.

To Greenfield	9	
New Berlin	5	14
Vernon	6	20
Mukwonego	6	26
East Troy	6	32
Troy	3	35
Sugar Creek	8	43
Richmond	9	52
Johnstown	3	55
JANESVILLE	11	66

(185) MILWAUKEE to WHITE WATER.

To Wawatosa	5	
Brookfield	6	11
Waukesha	5	16
Genesee	8	24
Ottawa	6	30
Palmyra	8	38
WHITE WATER	10	48

(186) MILWAUKEE to FOND DU LAC.

To Granville	10	
Menominee Falls	7	17
Polk	20	37
Hamer	7	44
Theresa	8	52
Springfield	6	58
Byron	5	63
FOND DU LAC	8	71

(187) MILWAUKEE to SHEBOYGAN.

To Good Hope	8	
Mequon River	6	14
Cedarburg	6	20
Grafton	3	23
Sackville	4	27
Ozaukie	4	31
Cedar Grove	12	43
Gibbville	6	49
Sheboygan Falls	6	55
SHEBOYGAN	6	61

(188) MILWAUKEE to SHEBOYGAN.

Steamboat.

To Ozaukie	28	
SHEBOYGAN	30	58

(189) RACINE to JANESVILLE.

To Fountain	7	
Ives' Grove	8	15
Yorkville	5	20
Rochester	4	24
Burlington	5	29
Spring Prairie	7	36
Elkhorn	8	44
Delevan	6	50
Darien	4	54
Fairfield	3	57
Emerald Grove	7	64
JANESVILLE	8	72

(190) SOUTHPORT to BELOIT.

To Pleasant Prairie	4	
Bristol	6	10
Salem	9	19
Geneva	15	34
Geneva Bay	6	40
Walworth	4	44
Sharon	6	50
Allen's Grove	3	53
Clinton	6	59
BELOIT	9	68

(191) JANESVILLE to FOND DU LAC.

To Milton	8	
Koskonong	8	16
Fort Atkinson	5	21
Jefferson	6	27
Johnson's Creek	5	32
WATERTOWN	10	42
Emmet	5	47
Clyman	3	50
Oak Grove	6	56
Beaver Dam	7	63
Waushara	10	73
Waupun	10	83
Lamartine	9	92
FOND DU LAC	9	101

(192) JANESVILLE to GALENA.

To Bachelor's Grove	8	
Spring Valley	5	13
Decatur	7	20
Monroe	12	32
Wiota	12	44
Shullsburg	20	64
White Oak Springs	6	70
GALENA	10	80

(193) SHEBOYGAN to NEENAH.

To Sheboygan Falls	5	
Plymouth	9	14
Green Bush	6	20
Owascus	10	30
FOND DU LAC	11	41
Friendship	5	46
Oshkosh	13	59
Vinland	6	65
Groveland	5	70
NEENAH	5	75

MINESOTA.

(194) ST. PAUL to NEW ORLEANS.

Steamboat.

To St. Louis, (see 155)	728	
NEW ORLEANS, (see 154)	1212	1940

(195) ST. PAUL to FALLS OF ST. CROIX.

To Stillwater	17	
Marine Mills	12	29
FALLS OF ST. CROIX	20	49

MILWAUKEE AND MISS. R. R.

MILWAUKIE		
To Wauwatosa	5	
Elm Grove	5	10
Powers' Mill	4	14
Plank Road	3	17
WAUKESHA	3	20
Genessee	8	28
North Prairie		
Eagle Prairie	8	36
Palmyra	6	42
Whitewater	8	50
Child's Station	5	55
Milton	7	62
Janesville	8	70

PRINCIPAL CANALS

IN

THE WESTERN STATES.

OHIO.

OHIO CANAL

Connects the Ohio River with Lake Erie.

CLEVELAND to Rathbun's Lock	5	
Mill Creek	4	9
Tinker's Creek	4	13
Pinery Feeder	4	17
Boston	4	21
Peninsula	3	24
Niles	6	30
Old Portage	2	32
North Akron	5	37
South Akron	1	38
New Portage	6	44
Wolf Creek Lock	3	47
Clinton	5	52
Fulton	4	56
Wellman's Mills	5	61
Massillon	4	65
Navarre and Bethlehem	6	71
Bolivar	9	80
Zoar	3	83
Jennings' Bridge	3	86
Dover	7	93
Lockport	4	97
Newcastle	2	99
Trenton	4	103
Gnadenhutten	5	108
Port Washington	4	112
Newcomerstown	6	118
Evansburg	4	122
Lewisville	10	132
Roscoe	3	135
Adams' Mill	10	145
Webbsport	4	149
Hartford's	3	152
Frazersburg	3	155
Nashport	6	161
Licking Dam	5	166
Lickingtown	4	170
NEWARK	6	176
Granville Feeder	5	181
Hebron	4	185
Licking Summit	4	189
Millersport	2	191
Baltimore	5	196
Havensport	6	202
Carroll	2	204
Lockville	2	206
Waterloo	3	209
Rayneysport	5	214
Lockbourne	7	221
Holmes' Landing	3	224
Millport and Bloomfield	4	228
Circleville	8	236
Westfall	5	241
Yellowbud	5	246
Deer Creek	4	250
Andersonville	2	252
Clinton Mills	4	256
Chilicothe	2	258
Tomlinson's	6	264
Stony Creek	3	267
Head of Big Bottom	2	269
Sharonville	7	276
Waverly	4	280
Trimble's Bridge	3	283
Jasper	3	286
Howard's Lock	5	291
Cutter's Station	3	294
Brush Creek	7	301
PORTSMOUTH	8	309

WALHONDING CANAL

Extends along the valley of the Walhonding River, from Roscoe on the Ohio Canal to Rochester.

ROSCOE to Crooked Run Bridge	2	

Walhonding Dam	4	6
Warsaw	2	8
Bedford Bridge	2	10
Darling's Bridge	1	11
Gamble's Lock	1	12
Butler's Lower Crossing	1	13
Butler's Upper Crossing	2	15
Walhonding, (town)	3	18
Gamble's Saw Mill	1	19
Cummings' Bridge	2	21
Mohican Dam	2	23
ROCHESTER	2	25

HOCKING CANAL

Extends from the Ohio Canal along the left bank of the Hocking River to Athens.

CARROLL to Lancaster	9	
Reams' Mill	5	14
Rush Creek	2	16
Green's Mill	6	22
Hocking Falls	5	27
Logan	1	28
Wright's	5	33
Pattonsville	1	34
Seven Mile Run	2	36
Nelsonville	5	41
Monday Creek	3	44
Chauncey	5	49
Wolf's	2	51
ATHENS	5	56

MIAMI CANAL AND EXTENSION

Extends from Cincinnati on the Ohio, to Junction with the Wabash and Erie Canal.

CINCINNATI to Lockland	12	
Hamilton Side Cut	16	28
Middletown	13	41
Franklin	6	47
Miamisburg	6	53
Carrollton	3	56
Alexandersville	1	57
DAYTON	8	65
Tippecanoe	15	80
Troy	7	87
Piqua	9	96
Loramie's Feeder	3	99
Lockport	3	102
Newport	12	114
Berlin	5	119
Minster	3	122
Bremen	3	125
St. Mary's Feeder	6	131
St. Mary's	2	133
Deep Cut	13	146
JUNCTION*	35	181

* See Wabash and Erie Canal, Ia.

WARREN COUNTY CANAL

Extends from Lebanon to the Miami Canal at Middletown. Length .... 19 miles.

SIDNEY FEEDER

Extends from Port Jefferson to the Miami Extension Canal at Lockport. Length .... 13 miles.

ST. MARY'S FEEDER

Extends from Celina to the Miami Extension Canal at St. Mary's. Length .... 11 miles.

MUSKINGUM IMPROVEMENT

Extends from the Ohio Canal at Dresden along the valley of the Muskingum to its mouth.

DRESDEN to Simm's Creek	6	
ZANESVILLE	10	16
Taylorsville and Duncan's Falls	10	26
Rokeby and Eagleport	10	36
McConnellsville and Malta	7	43
Windsor	10	53
Luke's Chute	5	58
Beverly and Waterford	10	68
Lowell	11	79
Devoll's	7	86
MARIETTA and HAMAR	5	91

SANDY AND BEAVER CANAL

(Mahoning)

Extends from the Ohio Canal at Bolivar, along the valleys of the Sandy and Beaver Creeks to the Ohio River. Length . . 86 miles.

INDIANA.

WABASH AND ERIE CANAL.

Ohio Division.

Manhattan to TOLEDO	4	
Port Miami	8	12
Maumee City	1	13
Waterville	5	18
Otsego	7	25

Providence	5	30
Damascus	6	36
Napoleon	8	44
Florida	8	52
Independence	5	57
DEFIANCE	4	61
Junction of Miami Extension Canal	9	70
Reservoir	11	81
Antwerp	3	84
State Line	4	88
Indiana Division.		
Indiana City	3	91
Fairport	2	93
Lewiston	3	96
FORT WAYNE	12	108
Aboité	11	119
Huntington	16	135
Utica	9	144
Lagro	5	149
WABASH	6	155
Peru	15	170
Lewisburg	8	178
LOGANSPORT	8	186
Amsterdam	9	195
Lockport	6	201
Carrollton	6	207
Delphi	5	212
Americus	8	220
LA FAYETTE	10	230
Lodi or Coal Creek	51	281
TERRE HAUTE	36	317
Point Commerce*	42	359
Newburg	17	376
Pigeon Dam	72	448
EVANSVILLE	19	467

* This canal is now open to Point Commerce.

WHITEWATER CANAL.

This canal extends from Cambridge on the National Road to the Ohio River.

LAWRENCEBURG to Hardingsburg		
Elizabethtown	6	
Harrison	8	14
New Trenton	6	20
Brookville	11	31
Laurel City	14	45
Connersville	11	56
CAMBRIDGE	12	68

ILLINOIS.

ILLINOIS AND MICHIGAN CANAL

Extends from Lake Michigan to Peru on the Illinois River, thereby opening a water communication between the Lake and Mississippi River.

CHICAGO to Canalport	4	
Summit	8	12
Des Plaines	10	22
Athens	4	26
Lockport	6	32
JOLIET	6	38
Dupage	10	48
Dresden	4	52
Morrisiana	9	61
Clarkson	4	65
Marseilles	12	77
Ottawa	8	85
Utica	9	94
La Salle	4	98
PERU	2	100

TABLE OF UNITED STATES AND FOREIGN MONEYS

UNITED STATES' MONEYS.

		Fineness.	*Weight.*		*Value.*	
GOLD.—	Washington	$\frac{900}{1000}$ *	516	grains	20	dollars.
	Eagle	"	258	"	10	"
	½ Eagle	"	129	"	5	"
	¼ Eagle	"	61.5	"	2½	"
	Dollar	"	25.8	"	1	"
SILVER.—	Dollar	$\frac{900}{1000}$ †	412.5	"	100	cents
	½ Dollar	"	206.25	"	50	"
	¼ Dollar	"	103.125	"	25	"
	Dime	"	41.25	"	10	"
	½ Dime	"	20.625	"	5	"
COPPER.—	Cent	pure	168	"	10	mills.‡
	½ Cent	"	84	"	5	"

Accounts are kept in dollars, ($,) cents, (c.) and mills, (m.) The Spanish silver dollar and its parts, (1-2s., 1-4ths, 1-8ths, and 1-16ths;) and also those of Mexico and the South American republics, circulate at the same values as the U. S. dollar and its parts. The gold of Spain, Mexico, and the South American republics has a legal value of 89.9 cents per dwt. In retail trade the dollar is variously divided in different states: in New York it is divided into shillings=12½ cents, and sixpences=6¼ cents; in New England into shillings also, but the shilling there is 16 2-3 cents, and the New York shilling (which corresponds with the Spanish *eighth*) is 9 pence, and so in proportion. In the Southern States the Spanish *eighth* is called a *bit*, and the *sixteenth* a *fip* or *picayune*, and are taken as 10 and 5 cents. The greatest bulk of the circulating medium in the United States consists of notes of a dollar and upwards, issued by banks incorporated under the sanction of the individual states.

FOREIGN MONEYS,

And their equivalents in United States' currency.

Gold Coins.

Coin	Value	Coin	Value
British Sovereign	$4 84	*Prussian* 10 Thalers	$7 82
" Guinea	5 00	*Cologne* Ducat	2 24¾
French Napoleon	3 83	*Danish* Ducat	2 25
" Louis d'or	4 50	" Frederick d'or	3 90
Spanish Doubloon	15 93	*Frankfort* Ducat	2 26
" " Patriot	15 00	*Geneva* Pistole (old)	3 95¾
Portuguese Dobraon	34 00	" " (new)	3 40½
" Crown	5 80	*Russian* Ruble	3 90
Holland Ducat	2 26	*Italian* Pistole	3 85
Austrian Ducat	2 28¾		

Silver Coins.

Coin	Value	Coin	Value
British Crown	$1 15	*Bremen* 48 grotes	$ 55
" Shilling	23	" Rix Dollar	78¾
" Sixpence	11	*Hamburg* "	1 08½
French Franc	18¾	*Hanoverian* " (constitution)	1 08
Spanish Dollar	1 03	*Holland* Florin	40
" Pistareen: head 18—cross.	16	*Belgic* " (1790)	34½
Portuguese Crusado	50	" " (1816)	41½
Austrian Rix Dollar (1800)	99¾	" Franc	18¾
" " (Hungary)	1 01½	*Prussian* Rix Dollar (currency)	69
" Florin	48½	" " (convention)	1 01¾
Bavarian Rix Dollar	97	" Thaler	69½
Brunswick "	1 00¾	*Russian* Ruble	73
Danish " (Schleswic, &c.)	1 06	*Saxony* Rix Dollar (convention)	1 00¾
" Specie Dollar	1 05	" " (Leipsic)	69
Swedish "	1 06	*Sicilian* Scudo	97¾
Swiss Ecu or "	1 01½		

Pound currency of British provinces in America=$4.

* The alloy, silver and copper—the silver not to exceed one half. † The alloy is copper.
‡ The *mill* is an imaginary coin, being the 1000th part of a dollar.

CATALOGUE

OF

MAPS, CHARTS, BOOKS, ETC.,

PUBLISHED BY

J. H. COLTON & CO.,

NO. 172 WILLIAM-STREET, CORNER OF BEEKMAN

Illustrated and Embellished Steel-Plate

MAP OF THE WORLD,

On Mercator's Projection, exhibiting the recent Arctic and Antarctic Discoveries and Explorations, &c. &c. 6 sheets. Size, 80 by 60 inches.

Price, mounted, $10 00.

This splendid and highly-finished map is the largest and most accurate work of the kind ever published. It exhibits a full *resumé* of all geographical knowledge, and shows at one view, not only the world as it *now* is, in all its natural and political relations, but also the progress of discovery from the earliest ages. In its compilation, every facility has been rendered by the liberality of our own government in furnishing published and private maps and documents; and also by the governments of Europe, especially those of France and England, whose rich stores of geographical works have elicited much, that until the present publication has been as a sealed letter. As a work of art, it excels all its predecessors, and is as ornamental as useful. It is beautifully colored, and mounted in the handsomest style.

MAP OF THE WORLD,

On Mercator's Projection, exhibiting the recent Arctic and Antarctic Discoveries and Explorations, &c. &c. 2 sheets. Size, 44 by 36 inches.

Price, mounted, $3 00.

This work is reduced from the large map, and contains all the more important features of that publication. It has been constructed with especial reference to commercial utility; the ports, lines of travel, interior trading towns and posts, &c., being accurately laid down. An important feature in this map is the transposition of the continents so as to give America a central position, and exhibit the Atlantic and Pacific oceans in their entirety. The map is engraved on steel, highly embellished, and mounted in the best style. As a medium sized map, it contains much more than the usual amount of information.

MAP OF THE WORLD,

On Mercator's projection, &c. 1 sheet. Size, 28 by 22 inches. Price, mounted, $1 50.

This is a beautifully got up map, and, from the closeness of its information, contains as much as the generality of maps twice its size. It is well adapted for the use of those who do not require the detail of topography, which is the peculiar feature in the larger maps. As a companion to the student of general history it is, perhaps, preferable to any other, as it is compact and easy of reference. The progress of discovery, from the times of Columbus to the present day, is fully exhibited; and especial care has been taken to show distinctly the recent explorations in the Arctic and Antarctic regions.

MISSIONARY MAP OF THE WORLD,

On a hemispherical projection, each hemisphere being six feet in diameter, and both printed on one piece of cloth at one impression. Size, 160 by 80 inches.

Price, $10 00.

This map presents to the eye, at one view, the moral and religious condition of the world, and the efforts that are now making for its evangelization. It is so colored, that all the principal religions of the world, with the countries in which they prevail, and their relation, position, and extent are distinguished at once, together with the principal stations of the various missionary societies in our own and other countries. It is so finished, being on cloth, that it may be easily folded and conveyed from place to place, and suspended in any large room. It is especially recommended for the lecture-room, Sunday-school, &c., and should be possessed by every congregation.

MAP OF NORTH AND SOUTH AMERICA,

With an enlarged plan of the Isthmus of Panama, showing the line of the railroad from Chagres to Panama; also tables of distances from the principal ports of the United States to all parts of the world, &c. 1 sheet. Size, 32 by 25 inches. Price, mounted, $1 50.

MAP OF NORTH AMERICA,

Compiled from the latest authorities. 1 sheet. Size, 29 by 26 inches.

Price, mounted, $1 25; in cases, $0 75.

TOPOGRAPHICAL MAP OF THE WEST INDIES,

With the adjacent coasts: compiled from the latest authorities. 1 sheet. Size, 32 by 25 inches.
Price, mounted, $1 50; in cases, $0 75.

MAP OF SOUTH AMERICA,

Carefully compiled from the latest maps and charts and other geographical publications. 2 sheets. Size, 44 by 31 inches. Price, mounted, $4 00.

This is the largest and best map of South America ever issued in this country, and the only one available for commercial purposes. It is also an excellent school map.

MAP OF SOUTH AMERICA,

Compiled from the latest authorities, and accompanied with statistical tables of the area, population, &c., of the several states. 1 sheet. Size, 32 by 25 inches.
Price, mounted, $1 50.

MAP OF EUROPE,

Carefully compiled from the latest maps and charts, and other geographical publications. 4 sheets. Size, 58 by 44 inches. Price, mounted, $5 00.

The best map of Europe extant, exhibiting the topography and political condition of that continent with great accuracy. It is an excellent map for schools as well as for the merchant's office.

MAP OF EUROPE,

Compiled from the latest authorities, &c., with statistical tables exhibiting the area, population, form of government, religion, &c., of each state. 1 sheet. Size, 32 by 25 inches. Price, mounted, $1 50.

MAP OF ASIA,

Carefully compiled from the latest maps and charts, and other geographical publications. 4 sheets. Size, 58 by 44 inches. Price, mounted, $5 00.

This map is the largest and most accurate ever issued in America, and contains all the most recent determinations in British India, &c.

It is indispensably necessary to merchants trading with China, India, &c., and must be especially valuable at the present time, when our connection with those countries is daily becoming more intimate. Nor is it less valuable for seminaries of learning.

MAP OF ASIA,

Compiled from the most recent authorities, together with statistical tables of the area, population, &c., of each state. 1 sheet. Size, 32 by 25 inches.

Price, mounted, $1 50.

MAP OF AFRICA,

Carefully compiled from the latest maps and charts, and other geographical publications. 4 sheets. Size, 58 by 44 inches. Price, mounted, $5 00.

The largest and most accurate map of Africa ever published in the United States. It exhibits the most recent discoveries of travellers--the new political divisions on the north and west coasts and in Southern Africa, &c., &c. As an office or school map it has no superior.

MAP OF AFRICA,

Compiled from the latest authorities, and accompanied with statistical tables of the area, population, &c., of each state. 1 sheet. Size, 32 by 25 inches.

Price, mounted, $1 50

MAP OF THE UNITED STATES,

THE BRITISH PROVINCES, MEXICO, AND THE WEST INDIES.

Showing the country from the Atlantic to the Pacific ocean. 4 sheets. Size, 62 by 55 inches.

Price, $5 00.

Extraordinary exertions have been employed to make this map perfectly reliable and authentic in all respects. It is the only large map that exhibits the United States in its full extent. Being engraved on steel, and handsomely mounted, it forms not only a useful, but highly ornamental addition to the office, library, or hall. All the railroads, canals, and post-roads, with distances from place to place, are accurately laid down. To make the map more generally useful, the publisher has appended to it a map of Central America and the Isthmus of Panama, and also a plan exhibiting the inter-oceanic railroad, &c. It deserves to take precedence o all maps heretofore published in this country.

MAP OF THE UNITED STATES AND THE CANADAS;

Showing the base, meridian, and township lines of the United States surveys; the lines of counties, districts, and parishes; the location of cities, villages, and post-offices; all railroads, canals, post and other roads; also the district and town lines of the Canadas—the whole being compiled from the latest surveys and other authentic sources. 9 sheets. Size, 82 by 68 inches.

Price, mounted, or in portable form, $10.00.

OPINIONS OF THE PRESS.

"As a work of mere art, it is exceedingly beautiful; but as an accurate and faithful delineation of the country, in all its aspects, geographical and political, it is entitled to the very highest praise. The map is six feet by seven, projected on a scale of twenty-four miles to the inch; showing, with the utmost accuracy, not only the general, but minute features of the whole country. Every state, county, and township, within our whole broad territory, is designated by boundary lines—the courses of rivers and streams, canals, railroads, stage and post roads, the position of cities, towns, villages and hamlets, lakes and mountains, are laid down—every county being colored separately. The meridian and township lines of the United States surveys, and indeed all the topographical minutiæ ever found on maps, is here displayed. So far as the ornamental portion of this great work is concerned, we repeat that it is superior to any thing we have seen. It is splendidly bordered by scroll-work, and by the introduction, at proper places, of fourteen of the most important cities of the United States; among which, New York and New Orleans are most conspicuous, and upon a larger scale. Boston, Philadelphia, Baltimore, Washington, and Charleston, are very accurately represented, and beautifully engraved, as is the case with all the rest, Cincinnati, Louisville, St. Louis, &c., &c. These views, it seems to us, are worth half the price of the whole work, as specimens of our rapid improvement in the arts. However, it is to the *utilitarian* portion of the map, that we wish particularly to call the attention of the public. In this respect, it is invaluable."

New York Courier and Enquirer.

"This noble map is six feet by seven, projected on a scale of twenty-four miles to the inch, and is certified on the map by Mr. Steiger, the principal Clerk of Surveys at Washington, that it embraces all surveys made by the United States, from the Atlantic ocean to the American Desert, or to the 32d degree of west longitude. It would seem to be authority on all boundary questions, from national to township lines. This map is particularly valuable for its correctness in regard to the Western and Southern States and Terri ories. The base, meridian, and township lines of the United States surveys are given; and those owning lands in any part of our country, with the map before them, may put their finger upon any section, and see the streams, lakes, swamps, &c., portrayed from actual survey. In addition to the United States, the map contains a representation of the Canadas, and North and Central America, a desirable improvement upon the shadowy outlines heretofore given. The countries set apart by the United States for the use of the different Indian tribes, and their names, are also given. As a work of art, this map is unquestionably a high achievement. It is wholly engraved on steel, is splendidly bordered by scroll-work, with the introduction, at proper places, of vignettes of cities among which New Orleans and New York are most conspicuous, and embraces a fine view of our National and State emblems."

New Orleans Commercial Bulletin

MAP OF THE UNITED STATES,

THE BRITISH PROVINCES, MEXICO, THE WEST INDIES, AND CENTRAL AMERICA, WITH PARTS OF NEW GRENADA AND VENEZUELA,

Exhibiting the country from the Atlantic to the Pacific, and from 50° N. lat. to the Isthmus of Panama and the Oronoco river. 2 sheets. Size, 45 by 36 inches. Price, mounted, $2 50; in cases, $1 50.

The vast extent of country embraced in this map, and the importance of the territories portrayed, render it one of the most useful to the merchant and all others connected with or interested in the onward progress of the United States. It is peculiarly adapted to the present times, showing, as it does, the whole sphere of American steam navigation on both sides of the continent, and giving the best delineations extant of our new territories on the Pacific. All the railroads and canals are laid down with accuracy. There is also appended to the map a diagram of the Atlantic ocean, in reference to steam communication between Europe and America; and a detailed plan of the Isthmus of Panama, showing the several lines of inter-oceanic intercourse. The map is engraved on steel and highly embellished.

THE STATE OF ARKANSAS.

COLTON'S NEW TOWNSHIP MAP OF ARKANSAS.

Compiled from the United States Surveys, and other authentic sources. By D. F. Shall. Size, 30 by 35 inches. Price, mounted, $2 00; pocket, $1 00.

This is the best map of this state published—its correctness being certified by various government and state officers.

MAP OF THE STATE OF NEW YORK,

WITH PARTS OF THE ADJACENT COUNTRY,

Embracing plans of the principal cities and some of the larger villages. By David H. Burr. 6 sheets. Size, 60 by 50 inches. Price, mounted, $5 00.

This is the largest and best map of the state in the market, and exhibits accurately all the county and township lines; all internal improvements, and the position of cities, villages, &c. A new edition, embracing all the alterations made by the state legislature, is issued as early as possible after the close of each session annually, so that the public may rely on its completeness at the date of issue.

MAP OF THE STATES OF NEW ENGLAND AND N. YORK,

With parts of Pennsylvania, New Jersey, the Canadas, &c., showing the railroads, canals, and stage-roads, with distances from place to place. 1 sheet. Size, 30 by 23 inches. Price, mounted, $1 25.

This is an exceedingly minute and correct map, having been compiled with great care and a strict adherence to actual survey.

MAP OF THE COUNTRY 33 MILES AROUND THE CITY OF NEW YORK.

Compiled from the maps of the United States' Coast Survey and other authorities. 1 sheet. Size, 29 by 26 inches.

Price, mounted, $1 50; in cases, $0 75.

MAP OF LONG ISLAND,

With the environs of the city of New York and the southern part of Connecticut. By J. Calvin Smith. 4 sheets. Size, 60 by 42 inches.

Price, mounted, $4 00.

TRAVELER'S MAP OF LONG ISLAND.

Price, in cases, $0 38.

A neat pocket map for duck-shooters and other sportsmen.

MAP OF THE CITY AND COUNTY OF NEW YORK,

Brooklyn, Williamsburg, Jersey City, and the adjacent waters. 3 sheets. Size, 56 by 32 inches.

Price, mounted, $3 00.

The Commissioners' Survey is the basis of this map. The improvements have been accurately laid down: and to make the work more valuable, maps of the vicinity of New York, of the Hudson river, and of the cities of Boston and Philadelphia, have been appended. No exertion has been spared to keep the work up with the progress of the city and neighborhood. The exceedingly low price at which it is issued ought to secure to it a large circulation.

MAP OF THE CITY OF NEW YORK,

Together with Brooklyn, Williamsburg, Greenpoint, Jersey City, Hoboken, &c., exhibiting a plan of the port of New York, with its islands, sandbanks, rocks, and the soundings in feet. 1 sheet. Size, 32 by 26 inches. Price, mounted, $1 50; in cases, $0 50.

MAP OF THE CITY OF BROOKLYN,

As consolidated by an act of the Legislature of the State of New York, including Brooklyn, Williamsburgh, Green Point, and Bushwick, constructed from the official maps of the Commissioners and other authentic sources, exhibiting the farm lines and names of the original owners. Size, 54 by 40 inches. Price, mounted, $5 00.

SECTIONAL MAP OF THE STATE OF ILLINOIS,

Compiled from the United States' surveys. Also exhibiting the internal improvements; distances between towns, villages, and post-offices; outlines of prairies, woodlands, marshes, and lands donated by the General Government for the purposes of internal improvements. By J. M. Peck, John Messenger, and A. J. Mathewson. 2 sheets. Size, 43 by 32 inches. Price, mounted, $2 50; in cases, $1 50.

The largest, most accurate, and only reliable map of Illinois extant.

MAP OF THE STATE OF INDIANA,

Compiled from the United States' Surveys by S. D. King. Exhibiting the sections and fractional sections, situation and boundaries of counties, the location of cities, villages, and post-offices—canals, railroads, and other internal improvements, &c., &c. 6 sheets. Size, 66 by 48 inches. Price, mounted, $6 00.

The only large and accurate map of Indiana ever issued, and one that every land-owner and speculator will find indispensably necessary to a full understanding of the topography of the country, and the improvements which have been completed, and those which are now in progress. It is handsomely engraved and embellished.

MAP OF THE STATE OF INDIANA,

Compiled from the United States' surveys. Exhibiting the sections and fractional sections, situation and boundaries of counties, the location of cities, villages, and post-offices—canals, railroads, and other internal improvements, &c., &c. 2 sheets. Size, 43 by 32 inches. Price, mounted, $3 00.

This map is a reduction from the large work, and contains equally with that important publication all the essential features of the state and the improvements that have been effected. It is suitable for an office or house map.

A NEW MAP OF INDIANA,

Reduced from the large map. Exhibiting the boundaries of counties; township surveys; location of cities, towns, villages, and post-offices—canals, railroads, and other internal improvements, &c. 1 sheet. Size, 17 by 14 inches. Price, in cases, $0 38.

MAP OF MICHIGAN,

Map of the surveyed part of the State of Michigan. By John Farmer. 1 sheet. Size, 35 by 25 inches. Price, mounted, $2 00; in cases, $1 50.

MAP OF THE WESTERN STATES,

Viz.: Ohio, Michigan, Indiana, Illinois, Missouri, Iowa, and Wisconsin, and the Territory of Minesota, showing the township lines of the United States' Surveys, location of cities, towns, villages, post-hamlets—canals, railroads, and stage-roads. By J. Calvin Smith. 1 sheet. Size, 28 by 24 inches. Price, mounted, $1 25; in cases, $0 63.

MAP OF KENTUCKY AND TENNESSEE;

Exhibiting the railroads, post roads, &c. 1 sheet. Size 25 by 17 inches. Price, mounted $1.25; and in cases, $0.50.

STREAM OF TIME,

Or Chart of Universal History. From the original German of Strauss. Revised and continued by R. S. Fisher, M. D. Size, 43 by 32 inches.
Price, mounted, $3 00.

An invaluable companion to every student of History.

MAP OF THE CITY AND COUNTY OF NEW YORK,

With parts of Brooklyn, Williamsburgh and Green Point, and of Jersey City, Hoboken, &c. Compiled from the latest Surveys, &c. 1 Sheet. Size 32 by 20 inches.
Price, mounted, $1 50; in cases, $0 50.

This map exhibits that portion of the city below 87th street on a large and uniform scale; the portion north of that street is exhibited on a smaller scale, but is distinct and complete, being engraved on steel. The ward lines, fire limits, &c., are laid down with accuracy, and in every respect the map is well suited either for the office or pocket.

PORTRAITS OF THE PRESIDENTS,

And Declaration of Independence. 1 sheet. Size, 42 by 31 inches. Price, mounted, $1 50.

NEW MAP OF CENTRAL AMERICA,

From the most recent and authentic sources; showing the lines of communication between the Atlantic and Pacific oceans. One sheet. Price, in cases, $0 50.

MOUNTAINS AND RIVERS.

A combined view of the principal mountains and rivers in the world, with tables showing their relative heights and lengths. 1 sheet. Size, 32 by 25 inches.
Price, mounted, $1 50.

A CHART OF NATIONAL FLAGS,

Each represented in its appropriate colors. 1 sheet. Size, 28 by 22 inches. Price, mounted, $1 50.

AN ILLUSTRATED MAP OF HUMAN LIFE,

Deduced from passages of Sacred Writ. 1 sheet. Size, 25 by 20 inches. Price, mounted, $0 75.

MAP OF PALESTINE,

From the latest authorities: chiefly from the maps and drawings of Robinson & Smith, with corrections and additions furnished by the Rev. Dr. E. Robinson, and with plans of Jerusalem and of the journeyings of the Israelites. 4 sheets. Size, 80 by 62 inches. Price, mounted, $6 00.

This large and elegant map of the Holy Land is intended for the Sunday-school and Lecture-room. It is boldly executed, and lettered in large type, which may be read at a great distance. Both the ancient and modern names of places are given.

MAP OF PALESTINE,

From the latest authorities: chiefly from the maps and drawings of Robinson & Smith, with corrections and additions furnished by the Rev. Dr. E. Robinson. 2 sheets. Size, 43 by 32 inches. Price, mounted, $2 50.

This map is elegantly engraved on steel, and is peculiarly adapted to family use and the use of theological students. It contains every place noted on the larger map, the only difference being in the scale on which it is drawn. While the large map is well suited for a school or lecture-room, this is more convenient for family use and private study. Plans of Jerusalem and the vicinity of Jerusalem are attached. The religious and secular press throughout the country has expressed a decided preference for this map of Professor Robinson over all others that have ever been issued.

MAP OF EGYPT,

The Peninsula of Mount Sinai, Arabia Petræa, with the southern part of Palestine. Compiled from the latest authorities. Showing the journeyings of the children of Israel from Egypt to the Holy Land. 1 sheet. Size, 32 by 25 inches. Price, mounted, $1 50.

An excellent aid to the Bible student.

NEW TESTAMENT MAP.

A map of the countries mentioned in the New Testament and of the travels of the Apostles—with ancient and modern names, from the most authentic sources. 1 sheet. Size, 32 by 25 inches. Price, mounted, $1 50.

"Its size, finish, distinctness, fullness, and accuracy, make it very elegant and useful. Sabbath-school teachers and private Christians, as well as theological students, may esteem and use it with great advantage. * * * I own and value." *Samuel H. Cox, D. D.*

"On a scale neither too large to be unwieldy, nor yet too small to be accurate, it presents at a single view, with great distinctness, the scenes of the striking events of the New Testament, and cannot fail to give to those events a greater clearness, and by presenting so plainly their localities to throw over them new interest. * * * * * It seems to have been drawn in accordance with the best authorities."

Erskine Mason, D. D.

"Valuable for accuracy, beauty, and cheapness. Having both the ancient and modern names of places, and being of portable size, it would appear happily adapted for the use of Sabbath-school teachers."

William R. Williams, D. D.

"I have been much pleased with the apparent accuracy, and the beautiful execution of a map of the countries mentioned in the New Testament, published by Mr. Colton, and think it adapted to be useful."

Stephen H. Tyng, D. D.

GUIDE-BOOK THROUGH THE UNITED STATES, &c.

Travelers' and Tourists' Guide-Book through the United States of America and the Canadas. Containing the routes and distances on all the great lines of travel by railroads, canals, stage-roads, and steamboats, together with descriptions of the several states, and the principal cities, towns, and villages, in each—accompanied with a large and accurate map.

Price, $1.00.

ROUTE-BOOK THROUGH THE UNITED STATES, &c.

Travelers' and Tourists' Route-Book through the United States of America and the Canadas. Containing the routes and distances on all the great lines of travel by railroads, stage-roads, canals, rivers, and lakes, &c.—accompanied with a large and accurate map.

Price, $0.75.

MAP OF NEW ENGLAND,

With portions of the State of New York and the British Provinces. 4 sheets. Size, 64 by 56.

Price, mounted—colored in counties, $5.00.
" " colored in towns, $6.00.

This is a magnificent map, engraved on steel, and exhibits the state county, and town lines; all the railroads, and other internal improvements, and the general geography of the country—the whole on a larger scale than has ever been published before. It has also appended to it a separate map of New Brunswick and Nova Scotia.

EDDY'S MAP OF CALIFORNIA.

Approved and declared to be the Official Map of the State by an Act of the Legislature, passed March 25, 1853. Compiled by William M. Edd y, State Surveyor General. 2 Sheets. Size 53 by 46 inches.

Price, mounted, $5 00; in cases, $3 00.

Authorities.—The coast line from San Diego to Oregon and the Harbors, Bays and Islands, are from data furnished from the U. S Coast Survey Office at Washington, and includes the work of 1852.

The Salinas and Tulare Valleys, the northern portion of the State embraced in part of Siskiyou and Shasta counties, the Colorado River, and that portion of Oregon shown on the map, are from Surveys and Reconnoissances of the U. S. Topographical Engineers.

The counties of Mendocino, Trinity, and Klamath, are from the map of George Gibbs, Esq.

The country from the Pacific to the Gila, is from the map of the Boundary Commissioners.

The remaining portion of the State is from maps and sketches made by the Surveyor General, County and other surveyors, and from astronomical observations under the superintendence of the Surveyor General, and verifications from the U. S. Land Surveys.

The Mono country is from a sketch made by the discoverers, Lieuts T. Moore and N. H. McLean, U. S. Army.

WM. M. EDDY, *State Surveyor General.*

San Francisco, March 31st, 1853.

NEBRASKA AND KANSAS.

New map of Nebraska and Kansas, exhibiting the routes, settlements, etc. 1 sheet.

Price, $0 38; in cases, $0 50.

THE WESTERN TOURIST,

And Emigrant's Guide through the states of Ohio, Michigan, Indiana, Illinois, Missouri, Iowa, and Wisconsin, and the territories of Minesota, Missouri, and Nebraska, being an accurate and concise description of each state and territory; and containing the routes and distances on the great lines of travel—accompanied with a large and minute map, exhibiting the township lines of the United States' surveys, the boundaries of counties, and the position of cities, villages, and settlements, &c. Price, $0 75.

THE BOOK OF THE WORLD;

Being an account of all Republics, Empires, Kingdoms, and Nations, in reference to their geography, statistics, commerce, &c., together with a brief historical outline of their rise, progress, and present condition, &c., &c. By Richard S. Fisher, M. D. In two volumes, pp. 632-727. (Illustrated with maps and charts.)

Price, $5 00.

A CHRONOLOGICAL VIEW OF THE WORLD,

Exhibiting the leading events of Universal History; the origin and progress of the arts and sciences, &c.; collected chiefly from the article "Chronology" in the new Edinburgh Encyclopedia, edited by Sir David Brewster, LL. D., F. R. S., &c.; with an enlarged view of important events, particularly in regard to American History, and a continuation to the present time, by Daniel Haskell, A. M., American Editor of McCulloch's Universal Gazetteer, &c. 12mo. pp. 267.

Price, $0 75

MAP OF THE TERRITORY OF MINESOTA,

Exhibiting the Official Surveys. Compiled by T. Knauer, Civil Engineer, &c. Scale, 6 miles to the inch. Size, 32 by 30 inches.

Price, mounted, $2 00; in cases, $1 00.

This map contains all the recent surveys made in the Territory by the United States' Surveyors, and exhibits with accuracy the base and meridian lines, the county, township, and section lines, and the general topography of the country, until now so little known. It is the only authentic map of the Territory ever published, and will be invaluable alike to the emigrant the speculator, and the traveler.

PLAN OF THE CITY OF NEW YORK IN NORTH AMERICA.

SURVEYED IN THE YEARS 1766 AND 1767.

To His Excellency Sir Henry Moore, Bart., Captain-General and Governor-in-Chief in and over His Majesty's Province of New York and the Territories depending thereon in America, Chancellor and Vice-Admiral of the Same, this Plan of the City of New York and its Environs, Surveyed and Laid Down, is Most Humbly Dedicated by His Excellency's Most Obed. Humble Servant,

B. RATZER,

Lieut. in His Majesty's 60th or Royal American Regt.

2 sheets. Size, 44 by 40 inches.

Price, mounted, $5 00.

The value of the above map in legal cases is sufficiently attested by the the fact that the subscription list comprises the names of all the most eminent surveyors and lawyers in the cities of New York and Brooklyn.

THE STATE OF SOUTH CAROLINA.

MAP OF THE STATE OF SOUTH CAROLINA,

Compiled from Railroad, Coast, and State Surveys. By G. E. Walker and J. Johnson, Civil Engineers. 4 sheets. Size, 73 by 57 inches.

Price, mounted, $10 00.

This map has been compiled under the authority of the Legislature of the State of South Carolina, and is the only map of the State which, for accuracy of delineation and minutiæ of detail, can claim to be reliable. It embraces all the surveys made by or under authority of the local government, the surveys of the most eminent civil engineers in the service of the several railroad companies, and the results of the United States' Coast Survey; and for the authenticity of its material, and the general correctness of its topographical illustrations, the reputation of two of the most widely known and esteemed engineers of the State is responsible. Such guarantees for the perfection of a state map were never before afforded to the public. The map, in point of minuteness, stands unequalled: it exhibits the lines of all existing railroads, all railroads in progress, and those also which are projected, the whole system of post and district roads, and all other internal improvements; the situation of cities, towns, villages, post-offices, and the great multiplicity of other objects usually found on the best and most elaborate maps; and in point of execution, its artistical merits are such as to challenge the admiration of all whose opinion is worth recording. The large scale adopted by the authors, the distinctness with which its great natural features are depicted, and the truthfulness of its geographical context, adapt it peculiarly to the wants of all interested in commerce, internal trade, and general business within the State; and to surveyors and engineers it must supply much that is new, important, and valuable to facilitate their labors in the field as well as in the office. No resident, indeed, at all interested in the progress of the State, can well do without this map, which so faithfully reflects the actual condition of the country with which he is identified.

COLTON'S OUTLINE MAPS,

ADAPTED TO THE USE OF

PRIMARY, GRAMMAR, AND HIGH SCHOOLS.

This new and valuable Series of Outline Maps comprises—

A Map of the World, in two hemispheres, each 80 inches in diameter, and separately mounted.

A Map of the United States, 80 by 62 inches.

A Map of Europe, 80 by 62 inches, on the same plan with that of the United States, will complete the series

THE MAPS OF THE WORLD

Are nearly *quadruple* the size of any others now in use, and exhibit the different portions of the Earth's surface in bold and vivid outline, which makes them sufficiently distinct to be plainly seen and studied from the most distant parts of the largest school-room. They exhibit the physical features of the World, and also give an accurate view of its political divisions, showing the relative size of each, with their natural and conventional boundaries. In the corners of each map there are diagrams which exhibit the elements of physical geography, as the *parallels*, *meridians*, *zones*, and *climates*—the latter by isothermal lines. There are also appended two separate hemispheres, exhibiting the Atlantic and Pacific Oceans complete, &c., forming in all *eight* different diagrams, illustrative of the primary elements of the science. These appendices will greatly assist the teacher in his elucidations, and make tangible to the scholar the basis of geographical mechanism.

THE MAP OF THE UNITED STATES

Exhibits the entire territory of the Union from the Atlantic to the Pacific Oceans, and also the greater portion of the British Possessions in the North, and the whole of Mexico and Central America, with part o. the West Indies, in the South. It has also appended to it a MAP OF THE NEW-ENGLAND STATES, on a larger scale. The physical and political geography of this interesting region is minutely detailed. The localities of the cities, and important towns, ports, and harbors are denoted by points, and the map generally has been constructed on the most approved principles, under the supervision and advice of several competent and experienced teachers.

The Price of these Maps is $5 each

UNIFORM SERIES OF TOWNSHIP MAPS.

COLTON'S NEW MAP OF MISSOURI, compiled from the United States' Surveys and other authentic sources. Scale, 15 miles to the inch. Size, 32 by 29 inches.
Price, mounted, $1 50; in cases, $0 75.

COLTON'S RAILROAD AND TOWNSHIP MAP OF THE STATE OF OHIO, compiled from the United States Surveys, &c. Scale, 12 miles to the inch. Size, 32 by 29 inches.
Price, mounted, $1 50; in cases, $0 75.

COLTON'S TOWNSHIP MAP OF THE STATE OF WISCONSIN, compiled from the United States' Surveys and other authentic sources. Scale, 15 miles to the inch. Size, 32 by 29 inches.
Price, mounted, $1 50; in cases, $0 75.

COLTON'S TOWNSHIP MAP OF THE STATE OF IOWA, compiled from the United States' Surveys and other authentic sources. Scale, 14 miles to the inch. Size, 32 by 29 inches.
Price, mounted, $1 50; in cases, $0 75.

COLTON'S RAILROAD AND TOWNSHIP MAP OF THE STATE OF NEW YORK, with parts of the adjoining States and Canadas. Scale, 15 miles to the inch. Size, 32 by 29 inches.
Price, mounted, $1 50; in cases, $0 75.

COLTON'S NEW RAILROAD AND TOWNSHIP MAP OF THE STATES OF NEW HAMPSHIRE AND VERMONT, compiled from the most recent and authentic sources. Scale, 9 miles to the inch. Size, 32 by 29 inches.
Price, mounted, $1 50; in cases, $0 75.

COLTON'S NEW RAILROAD AND TOWNSHIP MAP OF THE STATES OF MASSACHUSETTS, RHODE ISLAND, AND CONNECTICUT, compiled from the United States' Coast Survey and other accurate and authentic sources. Scale, 9 miles to the inch. Size, 32 by 29 inches.
Price, mounted, $1 50; in cases, $0 75.

The above series is the most accurate and detailed of any published, and in all that relates to railroads and other internal improvements, is complete to the date of publication.

MAP OF THE STATE OF KENTUCKY,

Carefully compiled from the most authentic original maps, documents, and miscellaneous information. By Edmund F. Lee, Civil Engineer. 6 sheets. Size, 76 by 48 inches.

Price, mounted, $6 00.

This is the largest and most detailed map of the prosperous State of Kentucky ever published, and the production of one of the most accomplished civil engineers of the Union. It contains the minute topography of the State; the location of all cities, towns, villages, and post-offices; the railroads and other lines of travel, with the distances between places; the boundaries of counties; geological diagrams, elevations, etc., and statistical tables of agriculture, population, etc. It is peculiarly adapted to the purposes of all interested in the actual condition of the State, its internal improvements and general condition; and as an accurate and reliable map has no competitor.

MAP OF THE STATE OF GEORGIA,

Compiled from official and authentic sources. By Wm. G. Bonner, Civil Engineer. 1 sheet. Size, 26 by 19 inches. Price, in cases, $0 75.

This map is a reduction of the large map of Georgia by the same author, and contains all the peculiar features—detail, accuracy, and beauty—of the original. Roads of all descriptions, the proper location of towns, the county lines, including those of the thirteen new counties erected in 1854. are laid down; and the State throughout is represented faithfully as it exists at the present time. The traveler will find this map to be a true guide to the localities he may wish to visit.

THE EUROPEAN BATTLE FIELDS.

Map of Europe; together with a large plan of the Black Sea and Danubian Provinces. 1 sheet. Size, 30 by 24 inches.

Price, mounted, $1 25; in cases, $0 50; in sheets, $0 37

This map has been provided with the view of exhibiting the progress of the Russo-Turkish war. It contains a large amount of information, and will be found better adapted to its special object than any other that has been published.

MAP OF THE WESTERN STATES;

Viz., Ohio, Indiana, Michigan, Illinois, Kentucky, Missouri, Iowa, and the Territories, exhibiting the base, meridian, and township lines of the United States surveys; the lines of the counties; the general geography of the country; the railroads, canals, and other roads; the location of cities, villages, and post-offices, etc., etc.: compiled from the most recent and accurate sources. Engraved on steel. Size, 48 by 36 inches.

Price, mounted, $3.00; and in portable form, $1.50.

This Map of the Western States is the largest, most accurate, and, at the same time, the most convenient that has hitherto been published. It embraces the great features of the country, and exhibits, at one view, the bearing and importance of its relative parts. No one interested in the development of the West can well dispense with so elaborate a portraiture of its surface; and it will be equally interesting and useful for counting-house reference as it must be for the trader, traveler, immigrant, or resident, for which classes of our citizens it has been especially designed. In compiling this great work, it has been a chief object to have all the lines of travel, by railroad, canal, or otherwise, laid down accurately, and, in furtherance of this object, the assistance of the engineers of the several works has been obtained, and the lines have been traced from the original surveys by the surveyors of each respectively. In this respect, no former map of the West has any pretence to accuracy, and hence this publication claims preference with those who desire to acquaint themselves thoroughly with the country delineated, and its means of intercommunication.

NEW SERIES OF MAPS FOR TRAVELERS.

This series embraces maps of each of the United States, of the several British Provinces, and of Mexico, Central America, and the West Indies, exhibiting with accuracy the railroads, canals, stage routes, &c., also the principal cities, and other objects of interest, in appended diagrams.

	cts.		cts.		cts.
Alabama,	38	Lake Superior,	38	New Mexico and Utah,	50
Arkansas,	38	Louisiana,	38	New York,	38
California,	50	Maine,	38	North Carolina,	38
Canada East,	38	Massachusetts and Rhode Island,	38	Ohio,	38
Canada West,	38	Mexico,	50	Oregon and Washington Ter.,	50
Central America,	50	Michigan, North,	38	Pennsylvania,	38
Connecticut,	38	Michigan, South,	38	Rhode Island,	38
Delaware and Maryland,	38	Minesota,	38	South Carolina,	38
Florida,	38	Mississippi,	38	Texas,	38
Georgia,	38	Missouri,	38	Vermont,	38
Illinois,	38	New Brunswick, Nova Scotia, &c.	38	Virginia,	38
Indiana,	38	New Hampshire,	38	West Indies,	50
Iowa,	38	New Jersey,	38	Wisconsin,	38
Kentucky and Tennessee,	38				

NEBRASKA AND KANSAS,

Exhibiting the new Territorial boundaries, Indian claims, lines of travel, towns, etc., together with a map of the new Territory south of the Gila River. Size, 30 by 24 inches. Prices, mounted, $1 25; in cases, $0 50; in sheets, $0 37.

MAP OF THE COUNTRY 12 MILES AROUND THE CITY OF NEW YORK,

With the names of property-holders, &c., from an entirely new and accurate survey. By J. C. Sidney. 2 sheets. Size, 40 by 40 inches.

Price, mounted or in cases, $3 00.

WESTERN PORTRAITURE;

And Emigrants' Guide: a Description of Wisconsin, Illinois, and Iowa, with Remarks on Minnesota and other Territories. By Daniel S. Curtiss. In 1 vol 12mo. pp. 360, (illustrated with a township map.)

Price, $1 00.

Actual observation and great experience are the bases of this work; and in language and incident it has much to interest. It treats of the "Great West," its scenery, its wild sports, its institutions and its characteristics, material and economic. In that portion devoted to statistical illustration, the topography of sections and the adaptation of localities to particular branches of industry occupy a large space: the geology, soil, climate, powers and productions of each are considered, and their allied interests, their respective values and destinies, and their present conditions, are accurately described.

N. B.—A German edition of the "Western Portraiture" has also been issued, and will be found of essential advantage to immigrants from the "fatherland," as it contains all the information necessary for their gaining a knowledge of the states to which German immigration is chiefly directed. It contains an excellent township map.

Price, bound, $0.75; in covers, $0.50.

MAP OF THE PROVINCES OF NEW BRUNSWICK, NOVA SCOTIA, AND NEWFOUNDLAND,

And parts of the country adjacent thereto. 1 sheet. Size, 18 by 15 inches.

Price, in cases, $0 38.

A STATISTICAL ACCOUNT OF AMERICA;

Being a description of the geography, resources, industry, institutions, and other interests pertaining to the several governments and nations thereof. By Richard S. Fisher, M.D., author of the "Book of the World," and other statistical works. (Not yet complete.) 1 vol. 8vo. pp. 400. Price, bound, $2.00.

This elaborate work represents, in the tangible form of figures and descriptions, all the great interests which make and distinguish nations. It comprises among its subjects the geography, geology, and natural resources of all the countries of North and South America, and full statistical details of the population, industry, and general condition of each. It is a work which every American needs—sufficiently detailed in all its departments for the utilitarian, and in its style and general character not too elaborate for the college or school library. By the student it may be used as a sequel to his geographical studies, and it is perhaps surpassed by no other work in its adaptation for the family circle, as it combines with its subjects much striking and instructive information respecting the original inhabitants, the antiquities, and curiosities of the continents to which its descriptions specially refer. No one, indeed, who is possessed of the maps of America, ought to be without this work, which so lucidly fills up the outlines they depict.

THE NATIONS OF THE WORLD;

Being a general description of all nations and countries, their geography, resources, industry, and institutions; together with a brief history of their rise, progress, and present condition. By Richard S. Fisher, M.D., author of the "Book of the World," and other statistical works. (Not yet complete.) 2 vols. 8vo. pp. 400, 416. Price, bound, $3.50.

This is a work of universal utility, and, from its accuracy of detail, must become a STANDARD in geographical literature. It contains a full *resume* of all the great interests of nations, and describes, in concise language, the distinguishing features of the families of mankind, their origin, languages, customs, religions, pursuits, and characters. The vast amount of statistical information it contains has been derived from the most recent and authentic sources—principally from official documents referring to the year 1850, and hence, from the uniformity of the statistical series used in its compilation, comparison is more easy, and the results more lucidly portrayed. As a text-book for colleges and high schools, or as a work of reference in public and private libraries, it is invaluable, and in many respects its superiority as a "book for the people" generally is too apparent to be mistaken. It is in fact a companion to the Map of the World. It describes where the map *demarks*, and makes apparent to the mind what the latter only typifies to the eye.

INDIANA;

Its geography, statistics, institutions, county topography, &c.: compiled from official and other authentic sources. By Richard S. Fisher, M.D., author of the "Book of the World," and other statistical works. With a sectional map of the State. 1 vol. 12mo. pp. 128. Price, $2.00.

MAP OF THE SOUTHERN STATES;

Viz., Maryland, Virginia, North Carolina, South Carolina, Georgia, Florida, Alabama, Mississippi, Louisiana, Texas, Arkansas, Missouri, Tennessee, and Kentucky: constructed from authentic materials. 4 sheets. Size, 64 by 43 inches.

Price, mounted and colored, $6.00.

This map is engraved on steel. It is undoubtedly the best and most elaborate map of the southern section of the United States, and exhibits with accuracy all the civil and political divisions; the lines of railroads, and other works of internal improvement; the United States surveys in the land states, and a great mass of other information. Such a work the South has long wanted.

TOWNSHIP MAP OF THE STATE OF MAINE,

Exhibiting the railroads, and other internal improvements. 2 sheets. Size, 43 by 37 inches.

Price, colored in towns, $3; in counties, $2 50
in cases, $1 50.

This splendid map is engraved on steel, colored handsomely, and mounted in the best style. It is the largest and most complete map of the state it represents that has hitherto been published, and exhibits distinctly all the civil divisions, internal improvements, &c., with great accuracy and conciseness. In its compilation the assistance of officers of the United States Coast Survey has contributed much to the value of its representation of the seaboard districts.

GUIDE-BOOK

THROUGH THE NEW ENGLAND AND MIDDLE STATES.

Traveler's and Tourist's Guide-Book through the New England and Middle States, and the Canadas. Containing the routes and distances on all the great lines of travel, by railroads, canals, stage-roads, and steamboats, together with descriptions of the several states, and the principal cities, towns, and villages in each—accompanied with a large and accurate map.

Price, $0.75.

MAP OF THE UNITED STATES,

The Canadas, &c., showing the railroads, canals, and stage-roads, with the distances from place to place. Size, 28 by 32 inches. Price, in cases, $0.63.

STATISTICAL MAP OF THE STATE OF NEW YORK,

Comprising all the principal statistics of each county—agricultural, manufacturing, commercial, &c. By R. S. Fisher, M. D., author of the "Book of the World," &c. 1 sheet. Size, 32 by 26 inches. Price, $0 25.

Useful to all classes of our citizens, and indispensable for the information of parties engaged in the construction of railroads and other internal improvements, speculators in land, and persons designing to settle in any part of the State. All the material interests of the country are plainly indicated in figures on the face of the map, or in the tables which accompany it.

HORN'S OVERLAND GUIDE FROM COUNCIL BLUFFS TO CALIFORNIA.

Containing a Table of Distances, and showing all the rivers, lakes, springs, mountains, camping places, and other prominent objects; with remarks on the country, roads, timbers, grasses, &c., &c. Accompanied by a Map. Price, $0 50.

CORDOVA'S MAP OF TEXAS,

Compiled from new and original surveys. 4 sheets. Size, 36 by 34 inches. Price, in cases, $3 00.

This is the only reliable map of Texas, and being on a large scale, exhibits minutely and with distinctness the natural features of the State and its several political divisions. The following government officers certify to its accuracy and completeness.

"We have no hesitation in saying that no map could surpass this in accuracy and fidelity." DAVID S. KAUFMAN, THOS. J. RUSK, S. PILSBURY, SAM. HOUSTON.

"I certify to the correctness of this map, it being the only one extan that is truly correct." JOHN C. HAYS.

Besides his own publications, J. H. C. has constantly on hand a large assortment of Atlases and Foreign Maps.

Mounting in all its forms carefully executed for the trade, public institutions, &c.

25

AMERICAN STATISTICAL ANNUAL

FOR THE YEAR 1854-5.

COMPILED FROM THE MOST AUTHENTIC SOURCES

BY RICHARD S. FISHER, M. D., AND CHARLES COLBY, A. M.

The "American Statistical Annual" is a work in which are embodied the detailed statistics of all American States, and a summary of those of Europe, Asia, Africa and Australasia. The Statistics represent the condition of all the interests of nations and countries according to the latest official returns, chiefly those made since 1850. The work is divided into four parts.

Part First—contains the Census Statistics of the United States and of the States severally, and the reports of the departments of the governments of each, with abstracts of state constitutions and of executive messages; and among a multiplicity of other matters of interest will be found a correct list of colonial and constitutional governors, the statistics of asylums for the deaf and dumb, blind, and insane; school statistics; the financial condition of states; statistics of navigation and commerce, domestic and foreign; accurate lists of railways, canals, telegraphs, etc.; statistics of colleges, universities, theological schools, medical schools, law schools, and scientific schools; and statistical information relative to every interest of the states described. This division indeed contains a faithful review of the present condition of the Union and its component States.

Part Second—is devoted to the States of Central and South America, and contains the latest statistics relative to their condition. In its compilation the assistance of the ministers of the several states resident at Washington has been sought, and thus entire accuracy has been attained. No part of America has hitherto been so little known in this country as these states, and hence the information collected from such sources will be peculiarly valuable.

Part Third—describes Colonial America, and contains a vast fund of authentic information relative to the Russian, Danish, British, Dutch, French, Spanish and Swedish possessions, never before published. The late census of the British Colonies are chief features in this part of the work, and for these and many other valuable documents the authors are greatly indebted to the governors of the several dependencies. The Dutch and Danish censuses are also given.

Part Fourth—contains extensive statistics of trans-Atlantic States in tabular, form chiefly respecting the extent, population, finances, armed force, military and naval, merchant marine, railways, etc., of each. The conciseness of these statistics, which are all of the latest dates, makes them of great value for ready reference.

So extensive a work on statistics has never before been attempted; nor has such a variety of interests ever been brought together. The merchant, the scholar, the minister of the gospel, the physician, and indeed every class of society will find in it something of importance relative to his individual profession. The economist will appreciate it as a book of facts, and refer to it in his arguments against the sophist; and to no class of persons can it be of more value than to editors of newspapers, whose attention is frequently too closely confined to matters which preclude the possibility of research for a wanted fact, but which the index of this volume will readily discover.

The work is handsomely printed, in fine type, and contains as much matter as three ordinary volumes of the same size.

Price, $1.50 bound half cloth, leather back.

GEOGRAPHY AND HISTORY COMBINED

In 1 vol., 4to, with 80 Maps and 200 Engravings,

ENTITLED

COMPREHENSIVE GEOGRAPHY AND HISTORY,

Ancient and Modern.

BY S. G. GOODRICH,

Author of "Parley's Tales," and "Pictorial Histories."

This work contains 272 quarto pages, equal to 1,000 common 12mo pages: It is the most complete and comprehensive work for the daily use of Families, Merchants, Editors of papers, Lawyers, Postmasters, Emigrants, &c. that has ever appeared. It contains the Geography and History of every country, including the new census of the United States; it gives the situation and population of over 5,000 cities, towns, and villages; the materials are all arranged in the most convenient order, and a copious index serves as a guide to the history and geography of the most remarkable places in the world. This work has received the highest commendation at the hands of scientific men in America and Europe. (Price, half bound $2 00, cloth gilt $3 00, morocco $3 50.)

From the Washington Republic, May 5, 1853.

"This work belongs to the utilitarian class, and will doubtless take a permanent place in the higher schools, and in reading families generally. It is much more extensive than ordinary school treatises, as it includes some 270 quarto pages crowded with matter, and containing as much as two common 8vo. volumes. It is also illustrated with numerous engravings on wood, and, what is more important, with 80 maps, plans of cities, &c.

"It may be a question whether it is best to study history with geography, at the outset; but in a more advanced stage of study, there can be no doubt that it is desirable at least to review geography in immediate connection with history. This work is prepared with this view, and its introduction into the higher seminaries will prove a great advantage to education.

"But, after all, the work strikes us as likely to be most useful in families, and to general readers, inasmuch as it furnishes a very full outline of geography and history, with descriptions of country, so clear and distinct as to divest both of these subjects of the mists which usually attend them in the mind. They are rarely studied from the beginning in a proper manner, and hence there are certain labyrinths into which almost every one habitually strays in approaching them. In the present work, by a systematic arrangement, and especially by the use of numerous maps, ancient and modern, placed in immediate contiguity with the text the various topics are presented in a manner so lucid as not only to prevent new errors and correct old ones, but at the same time to render subjects interesting which might otherwise be unattractive.

"Beside all this, for general reference the work in question is exceedingly convenient, and will often save the trouble of consulting various sources of information. Take, as an example, the subject of Germany, with its divisions and subdivisions. In order to find the history and geography of these countries, as given in the book before us, it would be necessary to consult at least half a dozen volumes

"In regard to countries whose history go back to antiquity, the advantage is even greater. The view given of the Roman empire in connection with the Greek empire, furnishes an example of the remarkably clear manner in which the anthor has contrived to treat geographical and historical topics.

"We consider the work, as a whole, to be an excellent one, marking a great advance in the art of preparing books for popular use, and deserving therefore, universal encouragement "

NEW PHYSICAL AND POLITICAL ATLASES.

AMERICAN ATLAS,

Illustrating the Physical and Political Geography of the United States of America, the British Provinces, Mexico, Central America, the West Indies, and South America: constructed from official surveys and other authentic materials.

The "American Atlas" contains separate maps of every state and country of North and South America, and the West Indies, engraved in the most elaborate style, and colored so as to distinguish readily the civil and political divisions of each. The work embraces about 55 maps in *imperial folio*, and each map is accompanied with a letter-press description of the country it may represent; exhibiting, in a condensed form, all its great interests, industries, and institutions.

Price, $15.00; or without letter-press, $12.50.

ATLAS OF THE WORLD,

Illustrating Physical and Political Geography: constructed from official surveys and other authentic materials.

The "Atlas of the World" contains all the maps and letter-press comprised in the American Atlas, with the addition of between 50 and 60 maps and descriptions of the several countries of Europe, Asia, Africa, and Oceanica, and, in every respect, is got up in the same splendid style, and with the same regard to authenticity and correctness.

Price, $24.00; or without letter-press, $20.00.

The maps contained in the above elaborate works have been drawn under the superintendence of an accurate and accomplished geographer, and contain, besides the usual geographical outlines, true representations of all works of internal improvement, the lines of public surveys, and a great mass of other valuable information.

The descriptive portions of the work are written by DR. R. S. FISHER, author of the "Book of the World," and other statistical works. These descriptions embrace all the geographical, geological, and statistical information incident to the countries to which they refer; and also an outline of their institutions, political, religious, and intellectual. In the compilation of this, as in all other departments of the works, the most recent and authentic materials have been used, and the whole forms a convenient and reliable source of information touching the subjects treated of.

Works such as the above have long been demanded by the enlightened portion of the American public. For many years extraordinary advances have been made in geographical science; discoveries of the highest importance have been effected; regions before comparatively unknown have been explored, and their physical characteristics ascertained with greater or less minuteness; and on every side man has been actively engaged in acquiring information, whereby to extend the sphere of civilization and commerce. None of the important facts developed by these movements are to be found in the old atlases, and hence the necessity for entirely new works, embracing all the results that have been obtained from the sources indicated. The atlases above named supply this necessity, and in their maps and descriptions the world, as known at the present time, is represented with faithfulness and accuracy; and the vast amount of information collected by explorers, travelers, and others, existing until now in forms accessible only to the few, are incorporated into these pages. Every effort has been used by the publisher to furnish to the world works that shall be creditable alike to the genius, learning, and mechanical skill of America, and superior in every respect to any like productions of the press, either of this country or Europe. Their utility is not limited to any class, but is co-extensive with the sphere of civilized humanity.

LIST OF MAPS

CONTAINED IN

COLTON'S ATLAS OF THE WORLD.

1. Vignette Title.
2. Heights of Mountains.
3. Lengths of Rivers.
4. { Comparative size of Lakes. / " " Islands.
5. Physical Maps of the World. (2 *Maps.*)
6. " " " "
7. " " " "
8, 9. World on Mercator's Projection. (*Double*)
10. World, Eastern Hemisphere.
11. " Western "
12. Northern Regions.
13. Southern Regions.
14. North America.
15. British Possessions in N. America.
16. New Brunswick, Nova Scotia, and Newfoundland.
17. Lower Canada and New Brunswick.
18. Upper Canada.
19, 20. United States. (*Double.*)
21. Maine.
22. New Hampshire.
23. Vermont.
24. Massachusetts and Rhode Island.
25. City of Boston.
26. Connecticut.
27. New York.
28, 29. N. York & adjacent cities. (*Double.*)
30. New Jersey.
31. Pennsylvania.
32. City of Philadelphia.
33. Delaware and Maryland.
34. City of Baltimore.
35. Cities of Washington and Georgetown.
36. Virginia.
37. North Carolina.
38. South Carolina.
39. { City of Charleston. / City of Savannah.
40. Georgia.
41. Florida.
42. Alabama.
43. Mississippi.
44. Louisiana.
45. City of New Orleans.
46. Texas.
47. Arkansas.
48. Kentucky and Tennessee.
49. Ohio.
50. { City of Louisville. / City of Cincinnati.
51. Indiana.
52. Michigan.
53. N. Michigan and Lake Superior.
54. Illinois.
55. { City of Chicago. / City of St. Louis.
56. Missouri.
57. Iowa.
58. Wisconsin.
59. Minnesota.
60. Nebraska Territory, etc.
61. Utah and New Mexico.
62. California.
63. Oregon and Washington.
64. Mexico.
65. Central America.
66. West Indies.
67. South America.
68. New Granada, Venezuela, and Ecuador.
69. Peru and Bolivia.
70. Brazil and Guayana.
71. Chili and Argentine Republic, Uruguay and Paraguay.
72. Patagonia.
73. Europe.
74, 75. England. (*Double.*)
76. Vicinity of London.
77. Scotland.
78. Ireland.
79. France.
80. Vicinity of Paris.
81. Spain and Portugal.
82. Holland and Belgium.
83. Denmark.
84. Germany, No. 1.
85. Germany, No. 2.
86. Germany, No. 3.
87. Italy (North).
88. Italy (South).
89. Switzerland.
90. Norway and Sweden.
91. Russia.
92. Prussia.
93. Austria.
94. Turkey in Europe.
95. Greece and the Ionian Islands.
96. Asia.
97. Turkey in Asia.
98. Palestine.
99. Affghanistan, Belochistan, Tartary, Arabia, etc.
100. China.
101. Japan.
102. India.
103. East Indies, Birmah, Siam, etc.
104. Australia.
105. Islands of the Pacific Ocean.
106. Africa, N. E. sheet.
107. Africa, N. W. sheet.
108. Africa, Southern.
109. Cuba.

Whole number of Maps, 180, *on* 109 *sheets.*

TO TEACHERS AND SCHOOL COMMITTEES.

COLTON AND FITCH'S

AMERICAN SCHOOL GEOGRAPHY.

Now in Press.

J. H. Colton & Co. announce to the public that they have in press a new system of Geography for Common Schools and Academies, which they design to issue during the present year, (1854).

The wide spread demand for a new school geography, and the conviction in their minds that a great improvement on those in general use is needed and attainable, have induced the publishers to undertake the enterprise, and they are resolved that no pains or expense shall be spared in making a first-rate work.

Previously to undertaking the task of preparing a new school geography, the author (Mr. George W. Fitch) communicated with a great number of experienced teachers respecting the defects of our present books, and the manner in which the subject should be treated in order to meet their approbation. Profiting by the suggestions thus obtained, as well as by his own experience in teaching, he has sought to make the work eminently practical, and to adapt it especially for use in the school-room.

It has been a leading idea with the author, to give particular prominence to the facts of Physical Geography, and to arrange them in such a way that the learner may see the relations they bear to each other, and to the industrial affairs of mankind.

Great advancement has been made in this department of geographical science during the past few years, and the author is not aware that the facts relating thereto, with appropriate illustrations, have ever been systematically embodied in an American school-book, adapted to the comprehension of the great mass of scholars in our Common Schools and Academies. The author trusts that his mode of treating this branch of the subject will meet the approbation of all intelligent teachers.

The work is to be entirely new, with new maps and pictorial illustrations throughout. The maps will be nearly two inches longer and wider than those of any existing school-atlas, thus affording space for an enlarged scale, so essential for the proper delineation of small and populous states. They will represent the most recent surveys and explorations, and will exhibit the physical and political divisions of the globe according to the most recent information.

☞ The Publishers express the hope that Teachers and School Committees who contemplate adopting a new school geography, will await the appearance of this work before making their selection.

OUTLINES OF PHYSICAL GEOGRAPHY.

BY GEORGE W. FITCH, ESQ.

Illustrated by Six Maps and Numerous Engravings.

The Publishers take pleasure in announcing that they have now ready the above Treatise, designed particularly for study in common schools and academies, but adapted also for home instruction and general reading. The particular attention of teachers, school committees, and others is called to this work. It is believed to be the first attempt ever made in this country to embody, in a separate treatise, the more prominent facts of Physical Geography in a manner intelligible to the great body of pupils attending our schools. The scope of the book, and its general plan, may be seen from the following list of subjects, which are treated of with as much simplicity as possible:

THE LAND—Its Extent and Distribution; Continents; Islands; Volcanic Islands; Coral Islands; Mountains; Mountain Systems of the Eastern and Western Continents; Upland Plains or Table-Lands; Lowland Plains; Glaciers; Snow Mountains and Avalanches; Volcanoes; Volcanic Regions; Vesuvius, Etna; Earthquakes.

THE WATER—Chemical Composition of Water; Mineral Springs; Cataracts; Deltas; Oceanic and Continental Rivers; Inundations of Rivers; River Systems of the Western Continent—of the Eastern Continent; Lakes; distribution of fresh-water Lakes—of salt-water Lakes; physical differences of Lakes; the Ocean; its temperature, color, and depth; deep-sea soundings; Waves; Tides; Currents; Gulf Stream.

THE ATMOSPHERE—Composition of the Air—its properties; Winds; Variable Winds; Permanent Winds; Trade-Winds; Periodical Winds; Monsoons; Hurricanes; Moisture; Clouds; Rain; Snow and Hail; Climate; causes which determine Climate, Isothermal Lines.

ORGANIC EXISTENCE—Plants—divisions of the Vegetable Kingdom—distribution of Plants—Food Plants; Animals—their Classification; distribution of Animals, Zoological Regions; Man—Races of Men.

The Appendix contains several articles relating to the Chief Productions of Countries; the Exports of Countries; Trade Routes; Metallic Productions, etc. Also list of the Mountains, Rivers, etc.

The Maps which illustrate the book have been constructed with the greatest care, and, though small in scale, they will, it is conceived, be found sufficient to give the learner an accurate idea of the principal features and leading physical phenomena of the globe. The lessons are broken into short sections or paragraphs, so that the work can be used as a Reading Book, and questions are appended at the bottom of the pages for the purpose of rendering it convenient as a manual of instruction.

1 Vol., Duodecimo, pp. 235. Price $1 00.

COLTON AND FITCH'S

INTERMEDIATE GEOGRAPHY.

This book, which is now being prepared, will be a small quarto, and is designed for that very large class of scholars in our schools who wish to learn the more important facts of Geography, but who have not time to consult thoroughly a large treatise. The aim of the author has been to present in this work such facts, and such only, as every scholar should understand before he completes his term of instruction. Accordingly, all tedious detail and extended description are omitted; and the learner's attention is confined principally to the maps, from which only correct and definite impressions of locality can be obtained.

The Publishers would call the particular attention of Teachers and others to the Maps which illustrate this book. Every Teacher must have noticed that the Maps generally put into the Geographies for junior classes (commonly designated Primary Geographies), are extremely meagre and imperfect; many countries are not represented at all, and those which are exhibited, are delineated on so small a scale, and are so carelessly drawn, that the impressions they convey are of scarcely of any value.

The greatest possible pains are being taken with the drawing and engraving of these Maps. They will be very full of reliable information; the larger cities and towns will be in heavier lettering than the rest, so as to arrest the attention of the learner; and they will possess the additional merit, not found in any other similar book published in this country, of showing contiguous states and countries on the same scale. This is an important desideratum, and has been hitherto entirely disregarded in the preparation of School Geographies, the consequence being that no correct ideas of relative size and dimension are obtained, Other improvements are being introduced, and the Publishers feel confident that the Map illustrations will far excel those of any similar book.

PROGRESS OF THE UNITED STATES,

GEOGRAPHICAL, STATISTICAL, AND HISTORICAL,

BY RICHARD S. FISHER, M.D.,

Author of the "Book of the World," the "Statistical Gazetteer of the United States of America." Literary Editor of Colton's "Atlas of the World," and Editor of the "American Railway Guide," etc., etc.

A few years posterior to the foundation of the constitutional government of the United States, a census of the population thereof was taken under the authority of Congress in accordance with a provision of the fundamental law; and subsequently at the end of each period of ten years, similar and successively more and more minute censuses have been instituted. These enumerations have also embraced inquiries into the social and industrial *status* of the country, and its resources and wealth for the time being, with such collaterate inquiries as were deemed important to the determination of the economic and political relations of the States constituting the Union.

The first national census was taken in 1790, and the seventh and latest census in the year 1850. Intermediate to these decennial enumerations, the States individually have likewise made numerous statistical inquiries, which are still being continued at periods varying from two to ten years.

These show the progress of the United States from the first years of their aggregate existence, and, in connection with the annual returns published by the State and General governments, are the ground-work of the statistical portion of the present work.

The "Progress of the United States," however, is not confined alone to a statistical analysis of the development of the country. In its pages will be found a complete description of its geography, both in relation to the States severally, and also to the Union. The general history of the rise of the colonies, their struggles in the cause of liberty, their transformation into independent governments, and their onward progress, are also summed up, and their present relative condition and position in the Union fully illustrated. The subjects more particularly noticed are the mining, agriculture, commerce, and general industry of the States, their institutions of learning and education, their religious and moral institutions, and, in fact, all the great interests which make and distinguish their social, industrial, and political existence. Such are the various subjects treated upon: and certainly none can be more interesting—none more useful to the inquiring citizen. Without entering into minute and controverted details, which would extend his work to many volumes, the author has endeavored to exhibit clearly and truthfully the history of events, their results, and the high destiny that awaits the future of a country already distinguished among nations for its enlightened civilization, and the successful achievement of a position second to that of no other nation of ancient or modern times.

In One Vol., Royal 8vo, pp. 432, with Illustrations. Price $2 50.

COLTON'S
GEOGRAPHIC COMBINATION MAPS,

DESIGNED TO INSTRUCT AND AMUSE

THE FAMILY CIRCLE AND PRIMARY SCHOOL.

" *Utile cum dulce.*"

The series of Maps under the above title, and which are now in course of publication, will ultimately embrace Maps of all countries, as

The United States	**$2 50**	**The World**	**$2 50**
The Separate States	**2 00**	**Foreign Countries**	**2 00**

The design of the Publishers is to furnish an agreeable and attractive method of imparting to the young, at home and at school, a knowledge of Geography, and of blending amusement and instruction.

The several Maps composing this series are dissected and cut up into variform pieces; but in such a manner that each piece, whatever may be its shape, has a correspondence with the other parts of the Map to which it belongs. Thus from a score or more separate and differently shaped pieces a complete Map may be constructed.

The act of combining these parts exercises and amuses the mental faculties; and the study of Geography is thus made attractive, and more knowledge of the subject is acquired in one hour spent in this intellectual amusement than a month of hard book-study could insure.

Every family and district school should have at least one copy of the series; and simply for the reason that Geography can not be so effectually taught by any other means; and many an hour which a child would otherwise wear away in idleness may be saved to its advantage by placing these amusing instructors within its reach.

Each Map is packed in a handsome book-form case, and will form a valuable addition to the family or school library.

INDEX TO CATALOGUE.

TO

Authors, Publishers, etc.

J. H. Colton & Co. would suggest to Authors and Publishers that they are prepared to furnish Maps, Charts, and Diagrams, appropriate for Books of Travel, Railroad Reports, Special Descriptions, etc. Their material and other facilities for the proper execution of such Illustrations are abundant, and their arrangements so thorough, that works of this kind can be completed by them at a very short notice.

New York, *No.* 172 *William Street.*

www.ingramcontent.com/pod-product-compliance
Lightning Source LLC
LaVergne TN
LVHW021422110826
845150LV00007B/2047

9781425508647